QUANTUM PSYCHOLOGY:

Re-Thinking Time, Space &

Interpersonal Connections

By Isaac R. Betanzos

Edited & Proofread by Kristen Kennedy

Covers design by Bogdan Matei

Digital editing collaboration Andrew Tabash

ISBN: 9781699390948

"Behind everything great and magnificent achieved throughout history, lies a crazy and bold idea that only made sense to the person brave enough to pursue it. You are allowed to fail a thousand times, as all you need to achieve your real goal is to succeed once."

CONTENTS

PROLOGUE

What if I told you that the way we perceive time, space, and interpersonal connections, is misleading, even though their true nature lies before us?

This book summarises a body of ideas showing that Quantum Psychology can change the way we comprehend reality, the basic conceptions of which we have always taken for granted. This is an opportunity to question the very foundation of our essence and explore what *'being'* truly encompasses.

The moment is here and now, but the concepts of time and space can be elusive, as we will learn...

This is NOT a self-help book of any kind. If you expect me to inspire or guide you, stop reading now. I am determined to prove that the power to unveil reality and to write destiny is naturally inherent within each one of us.

This will not be a comfortable or easy quest; you may encounter frustration along the way and you will certainly need to move beyond your comfort zone regarding your understanding of consciousness and perception. Don't expect to find definite, set-in-stone answers; there will be none. However, you will find tentative explanations as we tackle, from a plausible and holistic perspective, some of the biggest riddles ever pronounced.

The theories and bold claims that I am about to expose are the results of years of introspection and self-research as, over time, I have fed my insatiable curiosity with all manner of odd and counter-intuitive topics. This book presents my interpretations of these topics and how they are connected, uncovering our position in the Universe as conscious entities.

Once you start this path, you will have to confront your beliefs. Expect reactions from *'strongly agree'* to *'are you fricking mad?'* along the way. At the end of the day, Quantum Psychology is about igniting your most existential and brave curiosity, to encourage you to start asking the questions that will apply only to you. After all, this book only summarises the answers that *I* found for myself after framing those inquests more systematically.

However, be aware that once you follow the white rabbit into the hole of your Quantum Self, some side effects might occur, and you may find yourself completely reconsidering everything that embodies this reality that we experience one second at a time; also inevitably, you will come out of this tunnel with a changed perception of yourself and your role as the main actor of your own story.

This journey will assist you, as it did me, in finding the means and context to further your understanding of the odd experiences and riddles that have puzzled humankind since its dawn. Furthermore, you might find Quantum Psychology as the perfect vehicle to articulate and identify the very core essence of your soul: where it comes from, how it influences everything in your life, and where it goes once this life ends.

Finally, and as the real ultimate goal, this book is a reminder to have present at all times whatever it is in this world that lights your fire. We all need to hold on to this ultimate and boldest objective, our *Venus*, the source of endless inspiration that raises us above the conventionalisms of our social and biological limitations. Because it is there, where we challenge and transcend the reasons and meanings of the common world, that we will find the true nature of our Quantum Self.

Are you ready to walk in a land where no one has walked before? Our path to change the perception of time, space, and interpersonal connections starts here; it is all your choice...

CHAPTER 1: INTRODUCTION

Have you ever felt that there is something about the way we perceive reality that *doesn't fit*? Like we may be missing an aspect of how the world unfolds to us? What if we weren't fully aware of our most basic and profound quality as beings, a quality which itself would help us understand the Universe and ourselves?

I want to challenge the way we have been biologically designed and culturally crafted to perceive and interact with our specific environment and society. We have undoubtedly developed as a species, thriving in this modern age and mastering the world around us, but parts of our fundamental nature have slipped from our conscious awareness. As this aspect of our nature slips through our fingers, we lose the potentialities and power hidden within that part of our souls.

As a conscious being, you may have questioned where our consciousness places us within this Universe and reality – is it an odd coincidence or an accident of it? What this book will present is how everything that we experience is deployed and influenced by a fundamental and intrinsic part of our awareness that remains mostly ignored and unexplored.

This central piece of our minds is the *Quantum Self*. Our Quantum Self connects the highest essence of ourselves with our biological existence, with society, and with every force and form of energy in the Universe. It connects us to the *Quantum Realm*, where the rules of time, space, and connection are radically different from what we instinctually perceive. However, far more significant, our Quantum Self allows us to connect with others at transcendental and meaningful levels.

The body of ideas and theoretical frames used to study the nature, implications, and capabilities of this piece of our (sub) consciousness is called *Quantum Psychology*. It is only through the perspectives provided by the holistic approach of Quantum Psychology that we will be able to tug at the thread of reality, unveiling the power our consciousness holds. Through this consciousness, we are given the essential master key that opens all the doors of curiosity and wonder. And, as a result, it completely changes the perception of our limits, grasping the importance of meaningful, interpersonal connections as a means of mastering and influencing everything else within reality.

Quantum Psychology connects all aspects of existence and reality. At its centre, we will find the raw, meaningful, and emotional interpersonal connections we establish throughout life. Experiences are as subjective as we are, impossible to accurately describe to anyone not sharing the given intrinsic and powerful sensation. As these experiences are universally identifiable, every being is be able to relate to that type of inner sensation, independent of cultural or social background, or even species. This is the most basic and crucial component, the very thing that enables us to differentiate life from the inanimate.

But why the 'quantum' in Quantum Psychology? Well, as we will explore in this book, the reason is rather simple and intuitive: that part of our (sub) consciousness, so elusive to us, yet so filled with potential, is not based on the same physical laws as our social and biological self. Unlike the macroscopic reality in which we interact and develop, the laws of *Quantum Mechanics* rule this core part of consciousness. Moreover, the reason for being so is quite pragmatic: just as the vast and magnanimous universe, our Quantum Self 'obeys' a quantum plane of existence, an infinite and eternal source of energy with odd rules and numerous particularities.

Although we will get into much more detail about the principles and rules of engagement in the Quantum Realm, for now let's just say that, at that level of reality, time, space and connecting is neither linear nor rigid. Quite the opposite, at this scale, the perception and observation of these factors is totally flexible, deceiving, probabilistic, and completely influenced by the mere presence of our own consciousness. Subatomic particles, which operate at this scale, seem to master time and space at their will. However, it is our Quantum Self that commands and governs the will of these microscopic and capricious particles. In the Quantum Realm time and space are, to a certain extent, at our disposal too.

Once you start digging into the implications and effects that our conscious mind has over matter in the subatomic world, there is no way back to perceiving reality as you did before. Pulling one string leads to the unravelling of another, and ultimately to the realisation that Quantum Psychology has the potential to answer some of the biggest questions ever asked: what happens after death, the concept of God, time travel, the meaning of life, teleportation, the origin of the Universe, and other seemingly inexplicable phenomena...

Furthermore, each one of those threads leads to an overwhelming common conclusion: pretty much everything we experience, interact with, or perceive, is interconnected and retro-influenced one way or another. There is a continuous energetic exchange between us (as individual beings), the physical world around us, and every living entity in the Universe – composed of the same basic ingredients as us.

When it comes to shaping and unveiling the reality we live in, our own (sub) consciousness is far more powerful than we imagine. Quantum Psychology reveals that there is another very important factor to take into consideration when it comes to understanding yourself, your environment, and the pursuit of your own personal goals. And, unlike other components involved, which have been widely studied and are intuitive to our biological perception, this one belongs to a world with completely different rules.

Quantum Psychology is about realising that you can use these seemingly peculiar laws to reach whichever goal you set for yourself. It gives you the ultimate power and responsibility for your self-development, through the conscious training of this part of your nature. Quantum Psychology is also, at a wider level, about opening new doors for social and technological development, taking our species to a completely new level, and changing the world as we know it.

The way we influence and shape our reality is greater and more flexible than we have been designed to believe. We have been made slaves to our own immediate sensory and perceptual limitations through natural selection and our biological instincts. But there is a part of your reality that is not limited by the here or the now. From this part you can access information about the possibilities of the future, or from other spatial locations, and optimise your decision making here and now. The compass to navigate this intrinsic power lies in the interpersonal connections we experience and the raw sensations they evoke.

Nonetheless, the laws of Newtonian physics govern the reality of our biological selves; therefore, unlike subatomic particles, we will never be able to play with time and space as we desire. However, thanks to our Quantum Self, we can continuously improve the tools inherent within us, and move closer to that reality. Just as it is unrealistic to run a marathon in under an hour and a half, no matter how much you prepare yourself for it, but through constant, thorough and persistent training you can get as close to that goal as physically possible.

Quantum Psychology is both the answer and the missing piece in explaining and connecting troublesome questions of life. It is the ultimate key to unleashing our unique potential as human beings. Like the glue that holds everything together or the conductor of an orchestra, this aspect of our nature allows us to have the sense of continuity of existence required for the Universe to persist in the first place.

Quantum Psychology is not exclusive to humankind. In fact, every single living organism in the Universe possesses some degree of connection with the Quantum Realm, as it is the basic ingredient that enables life itself. However, the range of awareness, or retro-influence, varies in qualitative and quantitative terms from species to species, from specimen to specimen, or even within the same individual over time. Picture it as a puzzle: every puzzle is made up of pieces; however the numbers of pieces, and the complexity of the puzzle, are not equal across all the puzzles that exist.

The story of Quantum Psychology is one of time, space and profound interpersonal connections, and how those three terms, the conception of which we take for granted, can be misleading, even when their true nature lies directly before us.

Everything great that you accomplish in life will be driven by a real, natural, deep, and raw sense of connection and purpose – even if it makes sense only to you. We all need the unique focus and motivation that finding our muse, our *Venus*, or our source of inspiration, gives us; that source can be a person, or a personal goal, or a life-changing event that gives you direction, meaning, and transcendence.

When you face a decisive moment, you understand that what you are to this world can be determined and written in a second of pure bravery and conviction. From there, it is possible to accept that nothing, not even reality, will overpower what you already know in your heart.

Right now, this may sound impossible to you. Hold that thought, for if you make it to the end of this book, the journey will change you. You may be filled with resignation, or realisation; but either way, I promise you won't be the same person ever again...

CHAPTER 2: THE WORLD OF THE 'BLINDS'
AND THE 'DEAFS'

You may be wondering to what extent Quantum Psychology proposes that our biological perception of reality is deceived in terms of time, space, and interpersonal connections. Let me present a parable that could exemplify how far our biological and social predisposition keeps us from full awareness, and from perceiving the complete spectrum of reality.

Imagine that you lived in a world where everyone is born blind. Sight would be an unknown ability for any member of this imaginary civilization. Imagine that every form of life has evolved interacting with the world around them in the dark, using only the rest of their senses – similar to life forms in the deepest of the oceans.

Since the dawn of times these species would have developed without being able to see, and in that hypothetical world sight wouldn't be required in order to thrive. Perceiving colour would be something too abstract to consider and comprehend. Wouldn't all the 'blinds' think that the world they evolved in and experience is the only one that makes sense, and anything else would be pure delusion?

Let's go one step further in our postulation. Imagine that, parallel to the world and reality of the 'blinds', there were also beings that, although they have the sense of sight, they are deaf and mute. Yet, as they can see the 'blinds' adapting to their environment using their own set of senses, the 'deafs' actively react to and interact with the actions of the 'blinds', shaping and retro-influencing their existence and outcomes. By interfering now and then, they could choose to influence their destiny. However, the default sensory systems of both civilizations wouldn't allow them to communicate with each other in biologically natural ways, and would prevent them from ever being fully aware of their interconnection and the affects on their lives. They would share the same world, yet belong to different realities.

How would the 'blinds' interpret the interventions of the 'deafs', since their default sensory setting would allow limited perception of reality? Most likely, and depending on how evolved the 'blinds' might be, they might explain those phenomena in a similar way to how our theological, philosophical, or pseudo-psychological approaches do. Many of them would choose to attribute those unexplainable sensory situations to external, uncontrollable, and divine forces. Some would also believe that this external power is pre-determined and that they have little or no power to influence or interact with this higher entity.

In a more advanced civilization, they might attempt to tackle the riddle from a scientific perspective, but would still be limited by the boundaries of their perception of reality. They may be able to move in the right direction, feeling that something is escaping their senses, yet would be unable to experience it from a subjective perspective, or fully explain it scientifically. The totality of reality would be too complicated and abstract to be comprehended by someone incapable of questioning the very foundations of their existence. Without the understanding of what sight is, a piece of this complex puzzle would be missing. Yet, for the 'deafs' perceiving this layer of reality would be easy and natural.

Let's go another step further: imagine that you were part of the 'blinds' society, but born with the unique blessing of sight, alongside all the other senses. You would be able to perceive all the colours of the world, scents, sounds, and tastes... And, what's more important, you would be able to perceive that your reality is shared with the 'deafs'. This key, missing piece, would explain all the riddles and odd experiences that others had attempted to explain through religion or deductive ways.

With this unique understanding of reality you would be able to rationalise what, up until then, was a body of irrational and pseudoscientific beliefs, which were partially true, but mostly mistaken. You would understand that the decision to influence your own reality comes mostly from within, and not from divine, uncontrollable power. And you may even comprehend the infinite potentiality that lies within each one of the 'blinds', through their unknown ability to interact with the 'deafs'.

However, how would you ever explain the colours, or what the *real* world looks like, to those who have no comprehension that their perception of reality is limited? Especially when that limited perception is enough to keep them living, procreating and explaining the basics of the world they interact with?

You would be aware of how the blinds are all interconnected with the 'deafs', and how their actions influence each other. And, throughout your life, you would know that you interact and perceive the world differently to how everyone else around you does. Therefore, you would be conscious that acknowledging and exploring this wider version of reality would bring the whole species a step forward.

Undoubtedly you would face resistance amongst the 'blinds' who, without the perception and sense to understand the wider reality, would not want to give up their erroneous ideas about the configuration of the world. Many of them would be satisfied with their simplified perception of reality and may even be willing to fight and die, in order to preserve their ideas. Perhaps understandable, as being right is one of the most powerful psychological principles. Even the scientific community of the 'blinds', who dedicated their lives to understand reality would be reluctant to believe the truth, especially when they cannot experience it with their own senses.

As you probably guessed, the 'blinds' of the parable would be humankind, experiencing reality according to the limited perception of the five main senses. The 'deafs' would correspond to the subatomic quantum realm. Understanding Quantum Psychology would be like being a 'blind' individual that is able to see. Quantum Psychology postulates that a part of our consciousness interacts with this higher dimension of reality, where time, space, and connections unfold in a very different way to how we perceive it. This very same part of our (sub) consciousness, our Quantum Self, acts as the bridge between both interconnected realities.

As we will cover in the upcoming chapters, since your actions and mind setting have an impact in the way the world unfolds to you, through Quantum Psychology you could influence your life and those around you beyond the biological limitations of the here and now. Ultimately your actions and thoughts have an echo into the past and future, impregnating the expression of the present with a reality made of possibilities and not of certainties, and driven by our consciousness.

This parable might seem an exaggerated example of what we can realistically achieve and expect from Quantum Psychology. Yet, these are questions and ideas raised to challenge your curiosity, whichever your field of expertise or set of beliefs. Because the truth is that the full extent of Quantum Psychology must be tested from very different disciplines and perspectives, from a spirit of mutual collaboration and communication. I know I am not alone in the world of the 'blinds', yet we are too isolated at the moment. With the help of those who truly want to see all the colours of the world, we will discover and promote a new understanding of how this perspective and reality have an impact in the universe.

Make no mistake: even though Quantum Psychology, and everything that can be achieved through it, might seem like an idea from science fiction, it is also the reality we live in, even if we cannot fully comprehend time and space like subatomic particles do. One day, we will be able to interact with reality without time and space being an impediment or limitation, changing our world and species forever. 100 years ago landing on the moon seemed like something humankind would never achieve, yet in less than 50 years it was made a reality, so too, what seems impossible now may become a reality sooner than we imagine.

Without getting ahead of ourselves, for now just remember: in every given important moment in your life, you face a choice, as Maslow said: *"to step forward into growth or to step back into safety"*. It might seem crazy, ambitious, unrealistic, difficult, lonely, and filled with risks of insanity and failure. Yet, you know deep inside that new understandings are worth the risk. You have to decide if you prefer to stay in the darkness and live a simpler and more predictable life, or experience all the colours of the world, fighting with all you have to share that overwhelming beauty with everyone else, even if there is no guarantee of success.

I will not lie to you, if you choose to leave blindness, it will be the most amazing and challenging quest you will ever set yourself on. But, as with everything that is truly great, it all starts with an idea that seems crazy to the rest of the world. The path to greatness, to transcend your own-self, may require you to sacrifice everything. But, right behind all that, you will find the real meaning of life.

Are you ready to open your eyes for the first time and perceive all the colours in the world, taking the responsibility and power over your own existence?

CHAPTER 3: THE LINKED CHAIN THEORY

How is the way you solve a riddle correlated with the number of times you get sick?

Most likely, these concepts seem to have no intuitive link. You are right; there is not a logical path directly connecting both events. This represents the basic and straightforward expectation of the natural 'action and reaction'. Unless you have experienced a very concrete situation, it will not be obvious to you that modifying one of these factors will influence the other, like some sort of cosmic butterfly effect. But, are our cognitive shortcuts being deceiving?

Let's challenge this basic assumption. If we look at the question a bit closer, a few commonalities between the statements can be found. For instance, they are both occurrences applied to you, and they both require your conscious awareness in order to respond appropriately to each situation. Despite these similarities, we are still far from finding any trace of causality between the two events.

When examining the question even closer, you will need to search for the individual causes and influences that can predict each statement. What if you found a common route, meaning that the change in one of them could indirectly, but eventually, impact the outcome of the other, and vice versa? Suddenly, the seemingly remote possibility pinpointing they are connected would seem much more plausible.

In fact, every single decision you make resonates through a massive and interconnected network of events, beliefs, ideas and physical factors, pulling and pushing one another throughout your life. All aspects of our (sub) conscious existence retro-influence one another to a certain degree, even if that influence is rarely experienced in a direct or unidirectional way. It is the individual differences between the weight, nature, and retro-interaction of those factors (or *links*) that cause some people to get sicker than others, to react differently when faced with the same situation, or even for a given trait to be most likely inherited in one family but not in other. However, to quantify the exact number of links, and correctly interpret their relationships, would be a titanic task.

If you were able to look through this network, you might end up lost, hypothesising about an aspect of your life that is totally unrelated to the original concern. But, if you stay on the right track, and remain focused on following the lead of causality, you might uncover a behavioural "chain" and discover where the initial and targeted *link* connects to the next one, then to another, and another... until you finally find an indirect, and perhaps counter-intuitive, connection between two distant *links*. Eventually, this realisation will allow you to mould your patterns of behaviour by modifying those *links*.

This is the basic idea of the "Linked Chain Theory"; a conceptual frame describing how different aspects of our existence affect each other, and how either the improvement or the neglect of some factors, has consequences on facets of our life that would appear to be unrelated. Understanding Linked Chain Theory is the prelude to grasping Quantum Psychology and what it means for your daily life.

The Linked Chain Theory falls within the revolutionary approach of Positive Psychology, proposed by Martin Seligman in 1999. Psychology originally developed therapies and interventions that focused on ill-being, intending to treat personality disorders. However, Positive Psychology switched the aim of Psychology to a research perspective based on well-being, focusing on the positive personality traits within a person, and an individual's ability to change their world with the right guidance. Seligman defined Positive Psychology as:

"A science of positive subjective experience, positive individual traits, and positive institutions that promises to improve quality of life and prevent the pathologies. Psychology should show what actions lead to well-being".

Positive Psychology focuses in valued subjective experiences from the past (well-being, contentment and satisfaction), present (flow and happiness) and future (hope and optimism), and the positive individual traits to achieve these states.

Another approach that contextualises the Linked Chain Theory is the Broaden-and-build model developed by Barbara Fredrickson. In this model, the form and function of positive and negative emotions are seen as distinct and complementary. According to the theory, negative emotions narrow an individual's momentary

24

experience, while positive emotions broaden an individual's momentary experience, initiating upward spirals towards enhanced emotional well-being. This model predicts that positive emotions accumulate and compound, such that the presence of one positive personality trait will stimulate the appearance of more, related, positive personality traits.

Positive Psychology suggests that a positive change within yourself can have a powerful impact on other aspects of your life. But, before we go into more detail about some of the main *"links"* or factors that shape your personality and interaction with the world, we should clarify a few things regarding the wording used to describe and visualise these aspects.

Firstly, picture each one of these *links* as an individual, yet interconnected, dimensional aspect of your being, which differ from one another at a qualitative, quantitative, and cognitive level. Whether we are talking about diet, DNA, hormones, immune system, psychological mechanisms, the environment... Each one of these factors independently contributes to your life; yet, each one is influenced by, and influences, the other *links*, or aspects, of your life.

To modify the nature of each *link*, you can either have a direct impact (positive or negative) on it, or manipulate another distant but interconnected *link*. When the effect is not directly applied to the *link* we wish to influence, the modification will most likely be weaker. The intensity will vary depending on the correlations between the links affected, as the effect of the change ripples out like waves, becoming weaker and weaker as they get further from the source.

Secondly, this 'cause-and-effect' process is not a simple chain, where one *link* linearly affects another and is only in touch with the previous and following *links*. In this conceptual framework, the *links* exist in an 'interactive network': they are interconnected and retro-influenced by one another, directly and indirectly. Therefore, this is an abstract cognitive and physical map of interconnected *links* with variable and dynamic weights shaping their correlations.

Thirdly, this conceptual framework is merely a theoretical approximation we will use to make the theories of Quantum Psychology more accessible. Under no circumstances, should the correlations between *links* that I use as examples be taken as set in stone. Although most of the correlations I will refer to have been widely backed up by science over 40 years of research, there is simply not enough data to make robust and conclusive claims for causality. Besides, the weight of each *link*, and its correlation with the rest of the chain network is as individual and subjective as your personality is.

Therefore, the best we can do is to talk about the "potentialities" of how one link interacts with the rest, but it is not an accurate standard, extendable to a wide population. To complicate things further, there are variations within each person throughout their life: a *link* might show a strong influence on another at one point of your life, but shift that weight in another period. The interactions between links should always be understood as dynamic, variable, interdependent and individualised.

To picture your individual Linked Chain, imagine a blurry and flexible network, where each link or nexus is connected to many others, but with different strengths. If you were to shake one of them, the vibration would extend in all directions, to every one of the links the vibrating nexus is connected to, these would also transfer that influence to the ones interconnected to them, and so on until the vibration fades.

The following sections will briefly explore some of those *links* (many more could be added) and how they

27

most likely influence others. This will set us in the path towards understanding what Quantum Psychology means to us.

3.1. Diet

The expression "you are what you eat," says it all. What you ingest, whether it is a balanced diet or a continuous flow of junk food and sugar, will have an impact on almost every aspect of your life – in most cases, this is an obvious and direct influence, in other cases, the effect is subtle.

If you think about it, your body is literally made of the food you eat; every cell is built from the molecules in the fuel you ingest. Therefore, the nutrients that you assimilate will affect the proteins coded by your genes, or the way they behave – if they have enough energy available, or if they need to take fats from storage, for example.

Moreover, what we eat affects the way our neurons behave, as our diet is their source of energy and will determine whether neurons are able to work vigorously and respond to the daily challenges of our demanding lives. This also impacts the quality of hormones and neurotransmitters our bodies will produce. An exhausted brain and nutrient deficient body will be chemically different to a well-rested and well-nourished one.

Our moods are highly dependent on the hormones working their way through our body, which means that the food we eat also impacts how we perceive the world, solve problems, cope with stress, perform at work, create and maintain healthy social relationships, and the list goes on.

Furthermore, continuously dysfunctional or unstable diet habits hugely burden general health and life expectancy. Needless to say, there are major health risks (heart diseases, obesity, diabetes), and benefits (longevity, a strong immune system, physical energy) associated with the type of diet we follow. Therefore, something as simple as deciding to eat a salad instead of a burger for the third time this week, if made into a habit, can help you live a longer and happier life, or achieve that promotion at work you have been working so hard for, or find and keep the right kind of people in your social circle.

However, a good diet for one person might not be the same for someone else. And, even more, a good eating habit for you now might not be applicable in the future. Diet is not alone in influencing your interactive network. And, as we are about to uncover, many *links* add their weight to the final equation that is your existence.

3.2. DNA, RNA, Protein Coding & Epigenetics

Our unique DNA sequence, contained in every single cell of our body, is the basic recipe for life as we know it. The genome sequence is an organism's blueprint, making each life form what it is; it is the set of instructions dictating all biological traits. The unfolding of these instructions is initiated by the transcription of the DNA into RNA sequences. The majority of RNA sequences originate from protein-coding genes (only some genes have the capacity to code proteins, while the rest seem to stand inactive).

RNA is structurally similar to DNA. RNA synthesis involves separation of the DNA strands and synthesis of an RNA molecule by RNA polymerase, which uses a DNA strand as a template. A protein-coding gene is composed of a series of nucleotide triplets – the codons – that encrypt not only the protein content but also the start and stop signals. Protein-coding genes can be organised into families of similar function, structure and sequence, according to their shared evolutionary histories.

In recent years, another important element has contributed to how we understand the way our cells and neurons decide which proteins to code and which DNA sequences are more likely to be passed on to the next generation: epigenetics. Epigenetics, as a simplified definition, is the study of the biological mechanisms that switch genes on and off.

Epigenetics studies the heritable changes in gene expression (active versus inactive genes) that do not involve changes to the underlying DNA sequence – a change in phenotype without a change in genotype – which in turn affects how cells read the genes. Epigenetic change is a regular and natural occurrence but can also be influenced by several factors including age, the environment/lifestyle, and disease state. Epigenetic modifications can manifest as commonly as the way cells terminally differentiate to end up as skin cells, liver cells, brain cells, etc. Alternatively, epigenetic change can have more damaging effects that can result in diseases like cancer.

Although our epigenetic marks are more stable during adulthood, they are still thought to be dynamic and modifiable by lifestyle choices and environmental influence. There are numerous examples of epigenetics that show how different lifestyle choices and environmental exposures can alter the coding of DNA and play a role in determining health outcomes.

From an evolutionary perspective, when it comes to passing on traits that improve adaptation and survival to the next generation, epigenetics acts as a faster filter than DNA. Epigenetics shows that the real power to affect our reality lies within each one of us, even with something as apparently fixed and determined as DNA. Think about the potential of consciously training certain traits and investing in developing yourself – as this can change you not only mentally and socially, but also biologically!

Epigenetics opens windows to further value ourselves and never underestimate how much we can shape and determine who we can become versus who we are supposed to be. Therefore, choosing how to interpret the events that affect your life, shaping the way we visualise and cope with the world, will not only influence our instant mental and physical health, but also the way each one of our cells work and what information about yourself will be passed on through your own DNA.

3.3. Hormones, Neurotransmitters & The Immune System

The human body maintains its homeostasis under different stress conditions with the help of the central nervous system (through neurotransmitters), endocrine system (through hormones) and immune system (through antibodies and specialised cells). All three systems work in conjunction to regulate body function and ensure smooth responses to the diverse situations of life. But what's the extent of their range and influence?

The Endocrine System and Hormones

The endocrine glands are spread in different parts of our body; they produce chemicals called hormones and pass them straight into the bloodstream. Hormones can be thought of as chemical messages or signals that coordinate a range of bodily functions. From the bloodstream, the hormones communicate with the body when they reach their target cell and create a particular change or effect in that cell. The hormone can also create changes in the cells of surrounding tissues.

The arrival of a hormone sets off a cascade of other signalling pathways in the cell and causes an immediate effect. For instance, insulin-signalling leads to a rapid uptake of glucose into muscle cells, or a more delayed effect, glucocorticoids bind to DNA elements in a cell to switch on the production of certain proteins, which then take a while to produce. An imbalance in one of the glands might have severe consequences to our mental, emotional or physical health.

Hormones control most major bodily functions: from simple basic needs, like hunger, to complex systems, like reproduction, and even emotions and mood. The body has many different hormones, but certain types play a bigger role in the body's health and well-being. For example, cortisol has been called the "stress hormone" because of the way it assists the body in responding to stress. Too much or too little cortisol for a prolonged period can have a negative effect on physical and mental health.

When they are in proper balance, hormones help the body thrive, but small problems with hormones can cause serious and life-altering symptoms.

The Central Nervous System and Neurotransmitters

Hormones and neurotransmitters are two separate chemical messengers, although there are some similarities. Some hormones, such as serotonin and dopamine, also function as neurotransmitters.

Neurotransmitters help to coordinate movement and control mood and cognition. They are synthesised by neurons and are stored in vesicles. Neurotransmitters are exchanged in the space between neurons called synapses, and spread out through the nervous system – relaying chemical messages between nerve cells and from neurons to muscles. There are four major chemicals in the brain that have been proven to influence our happiness: Dopamine, Oxytocin, Serotonin and Endorphins, known by the acronym DOSE. Without going into too much detail on each neurotransmitter, suffice it to say, experiences that release the DOSE neurochemicals make us happy, and we generally want more of what makes us happy.

Research shows that our diet is one of the external factors (amongst others) that affects which hormones and neurotransmitters are produced. This shows that something as apparently unrelated as what you eat, if taken as a habit, could influence a wide range of aspects in your life. This correlation is not unidirectional or stable over time. If our brain is used to generating a smaller quantity of the pleasant neurotransmitters, it is also more likely that, when deciding what to eat, we will turn to foods that give instant gratification, rather than making the effort required for a healthier option.

The Immune System

The immune system is the body's defence against infectious organisms and other invaders, through a complex and vital network of cells and organs that protect the body from infection. Through a series of steps, called the immune response, the immune system attacks organisms and substances that invade body systems and cause disease. The immune system, although partly innate, also evolves and adapts throughout life.

Everyone's immune system is different. Some people never seem to get infections, whereas others seem to be sick all the time. As people get older, they usually become immune to more germs, as the immune system encounters more and more of them. That is why adults tend to get fewer colds than children – their bodies have learned to recognise, and are more prepared to attack, many of the viruses that cause colds.

Research has shown that several *links* affect the body's immune system: poor diet, certain steroids, chronic stress... Therefore, how you spend your free time, your level of stress, how often you consume alcohol, how physically active you are, and even the air you breathe, can affect your immune system. This correlation can go both ways: for example, having a depressed immune system will also make you more likely to be stressed, have a sedentary life, and perceive the world in a darker light.

3.4. Cognitive & Personality Traits

For my Master's degree research, I ran an experiment to find correlations between certain personality traits and the way we interpret and deal with stressful events in our daily life. Although I will go into much more detail about the experiment later in the book, we will now introduce some of the cognitive and personality traits that affect the rest of the *links* in the Chain Link Theory.

The research showed evidence that our coping strategies, level of optimism, subjective well-being, and our style of attribution, are all highly correlated. Furthermore, when combined as a personality pattern, those factors were found to be a robust and strong predictor of a person's general stress level and sense of control when facing major or minor challenges in life.

When combined with other elements, such as body language or confidence, those traits play a vital role in our understanding of the control and power we have in life and in the way we interact with the world around us, both consciously and subconsciously.

Coping strategies

The term coping strategy was first used in the 1980s when psychologists Richard Folkman and Susan Lazarus defined coping strategies as *"cognitions and behaviours that a person uses to reduce stress and to moderate its emotional impact"*.

Most of the studies on coping focus on how an individual manages depression and anxiety. Different coping styles affect the way we perceive stress, looking at the perception of controllability, or positivity, of an outcome under different stressful circumstances.

One model to explain the coping process is the approach-avoidance model, which refers to strategies oriented either toward or away from threat. Researchers have found evidence that individuals using an approaching coping style habitually use an emotion regulation strategy that intervenes early in the emotion generative process, modifying the individual's behaviours and feelings.

'*Approachers*' show more adaptive coping by taking an optimistic attitude to any situation, and tend to score higher in life satisfaction or self-esteem tests. Contrarily, '*avoidants*' habitually use an emotion regulation strategy that intervenes late in the emotion-generative process modifying only what the individual expresses behaviourally. Individuals applying this strategy deal with stressful situations by masking their inner feeling; they tend to score lower in positive relations with others, levels of self-esteem, and life satisfaction, and present more depressive symptoms.

It has been suggested that individuals using an approaching style will be more likely to face stress as a problem to be solved. Instead of just worrying about their problems, they will take steps to deal with them, reducing stress and enhancing the perception of controllability. This type of coping tends to prevent negative events by modifying the life-context, creating the best conditions for actualising projects and ideas.

Tt seems improbable that coping styles can fully explain and predict the levels of perceived stress, and sense of control, during negative or stressful life events, without taking relevant personality traits into account.

Optimism

Over the past 40 years, there has been vast psychological research on personality traits on the optimism-pessimism continuum. Anthropologist Lionel Tiger provided an early definition of optimism, which stated: *"optimism is a mood or attitude associated with an expectation about the social or material future – one which the evaluator regards as socially desirable, advantageous and pleasant"*. The definition implies that there is no objective optimism, as it is individually evaluated.

In recent years, and under the influence of Positive Psychology, the relationship between optimism, other relevant personality traits and perceived stress, has been widely studied. However, research has shown that perceived control is also an important factor in understanding optimism. There is evidence that optimistic people cite more external than internal causes for negative life events than the pessimistic people. Generally, optimistic people report more perceived control over positive events than pessimistic people, attributing success to internal and stable causes.

Once again, evidence shows that positive emotions and personality traits accumulate, relate and compound. Therefore, people should cultivate positive emotions in themselves to remain optimistic, generating more positive attributes and personality traits in themselves and the people around them. This positivity is not an end in itself, but it should be treated as a means to achieve psychological growth necessary for overall well-being.

Subjective well-being

Research to understand and explain subjective well-being, a term coined by Alumni Distinguished Professor of Psychology (Emeritus) at the University of

Illinois Dr Ed Diener in 1993, has been present throughout Psychology as a science under different names (life satisfaction, quality of life, self-realisation, etc.).

Over the last 20 years, the concept of subjective well-being has evolved. Despite a large number of theories, tests and studies on the subject, it is quite hard to find a compelling and satisfactory definition for subjective well-being that embraces all the aspects of the concept. However, the following definition, proposed by Dr Rachel Dodge in 2012, manages to embrace simplicity, universal application, optimism, and a basis for measurement:

"Stable well-being is when individuals have the psychological, social and physical resources they need to meet a particular psychological, social and/or physical challenge."

This definition highlights the importance of personality traits and individual differences when interacting with a given context, and not vice-versa. With the upswing of the Positive Psychology approach, subjective well-being has come to mean being aware, not only of the positive events that occur in your life, but also that you are the cause of these events, that you can create them, control their occurrence, that you play a major role in the good things that happen to you.

Attributional style

The research on attributional style began over 100 years ago. However, in the late 1970s research lead to the claim that individuals vulnerable to depression make causal judgements with a tendency to view negative events as caused by factors that are internal (personal), stable (permanent), and global (pervasive). Over the following years, evidence showed the relationship between attributional explanatory styles, perceived stress, and subjective well-being.

Further, it was suggested that controllability is the most important dimension of attributional style-problem relationships and can be used to predict depression, loneliness and shyness. Accordingly, changing the perception of controllability over problems could also change expectations, motivation, and performance.

Positive Psychology proposes that an optimistic attributional style in positive situations is a stronger predictor of self-reported happiness than mental health. Additionally, in the last decade it has been shown that

43

attributional styles change over time, being susceptible to conscious training.

Coping strategies also influence the tendency to attribute positive situations to internal, stable and global causes, and negative situations to external, unstable and specific causes, impacting on subjective well-being. These biases are considered a healthy way to explain situations, serving to protect individuals against emotional distress.

Perceived stress and control

The way we perceive stress when facing a negative event, and the degree of control we attribute to our own capacity, can affect different aspects of our lives such as our health, professional or personal success, or even the decisions we make. Perceived stress is defined as *"the feelings or thoughts that an individual has about how much stress they are under at a given point in time or over a given time period"*.

From this perspective, perceived stress is not about the frequency or type of the negative life event itself, but about how the individual feels about the stressfulness it causes, and their ability to handle it.

Therefore, the definition appraises how individuals will face similar negative life events in very different ways. This is based on their personality traits, coping resources, and such, where the interaction with the environment is also important.

Similarly, evidence shows that the mere illusion of control significantly improves performance under different mild stressful situations, and it has been suggested that an individuals' failure to exercise actual control over an event might be compensated for by trying to bolster a generalised, subjective sense of control. Control might then be sought through acts where the effect on the environment is illusory. This observation led to the hypothesis that stress, which undermines the person's sense of control, would lead to illusory perceptions of controllability as a way to promote and protect personal general satisfaction.

Body language, your energy, and confidence

Body language refers to the non-verbal signals that we use to communicate. From our facial expressions to our body movements, the things we do not say convey volumes of information. It has been suggested that body language accounts for 50–70% of all communication. That statement may seem somewhat inaccurate and exaggerated, as there are so many factors involved in communication (verbal and non-verbal expressions, environment, memory, experience, mood, expectations and, of course, our personal energy and Quantum-self).

Nevertheless, understanding body language is important in order to reach a good level of communication and understanding, without forgetting other essential other cues such as context. In order to raise our own self-awareness regarding our body language and how we convey ourselves to others, we must include facial expressions, the eyes, the mouth, gestures, the arms and legs, the posture, personal space, intonation…

Once we master and control our gestures, the things we say with our bodies will help us reinforce why we are saying it. Further, paying attention to someone's body language can help us discern how someone feels about what they are saying, the intention behind the message or when someone is not telling us the whole truth.

Another important *link,* that connects us to our environment in a less 'observable' way, is our own energy, or what we express through our energetic field. Although it's quite an abstract concept to explain, it can be encapsulated in those moments when you might feel the presence of someone coming into the room even before any of your senses perceived it. Or having a dream where, despite not seeing someone's face, you just knew who that person was because you were familiar with the essence of that known person.

The energy we project to the world is both stable and dynamic: stable because there is somewhat of a base line of what our unique energy 'feels like' to the rest of the world; and dynamic because, as we grow and evolve as human beings, our energy may swift and change and acquire new nuances. Moreover, the energy we transmit also varies depending on factors like our mood, or even the time of the day, our general health, and stress levels. If you are energetically sensible enough, you may be able to interpret and detect variances in other people's energetic field, especially in those you know well.

When it comes to your unique energetic presence, once again, it correlates to, and retro-influences, other *links* in the network of links. In addition, this energetic field – that every single living organism possesses – helps us to connect and bond with the people we care

47

about. And, like any other sense, some people are more aware of their own and other's energetic fields. This sensibility can also be trained; either by conscious effort or by environmental pressure, as in the cases where a person becomes blind and the rest of his or her senses is enhanced.

Being very sensitive to energetic fields is quite a difficult sensation to explain to someone who is not. It is another factor, like body language, actual words, our experience and expectations, etc. that influence the way we interact with others and the emotional bonds we form throughout our lives.

As we will discover further down the line, this energetic connection can happen on a different sensorial plane, beyond our default sensory systems, connecting us with people and the world at a quantum level – or what I call *Interpersonal Quantum Entanglement*.

As the cherry on top of our non-verbal language and unique energy, confidence (not to be mistaken with blind faith) and self-esteem play a key part in the message you send to the world around you and how it responds to you in return. If you feel confident about yourself, in whatever situation you are, using body language accordingly, appropriate words, with control and awareness of how your previous experiences and expectations might be influencing the way you are evaluating a given situation, you will already be well on your way to succeeding in that particular situation or task.

Ultimately, you are in control of which version of yourself you project to the world. And, although you cannot control how others will perceive you, biased by their own experiences, expectations, and perceptions, you will always be closer to success if, whatever you are trying to communicate and achieve, you do it with conviction and confidence.

Our patterns of behaviour (whether adaptive or dysfunctional) are fed-back and reinforced in a vicious cycle, carved by our perception of the world, the substances generated by our brain, and the way each one of our cells work and react based in all the above. Your perception, and therefore the perception of everyone else around you, might be strongly biased and under the control of your subjectivity; the good news is that, if that's the case, once you are aware of it, it is totally up to you to break that vicious cycle and start a healthier one.

3.5. Heritability, Shared & Non-Shared Environment

We have covered how certain factors and traits help us understand the way we interact with the world, but what determines an individual's personality? Psychologists conducting research on this question have attempted to determine the degree to which personality is shaped by genetic versus environmental or experiential influences. We know, for example, that the individual differences in genetics are primarily responsible for individual differences in temperament. Research on sources of individual differences in the Big Five (a commonly used personality test) has found that genetics can account for about half of the variability that is found between people, reflecting an impressively powerful contribution of genetics. At the same time, the findings indicate that about half the variability is attributable to individual differences in environmental or experiential factors.

Heritability is defined as the proportion of the total variation between individuals in a given population that is due to genetic variation. It refers to the proportion of variability in a particular trait in a population, explained by differences in the genes. It has been widely studied shown that the variability changes in time. For example, when you are a child, variability in weight and IQ are more environmental, while as an adult this is more influenced by genetics.

But, what kinds of environmental and experiential factors are most significant as shapers of personality? Here, the findings from research studies have been quite surprising. Traditionally, it had been assumed that the most important environmental influence on a child's personality was the parenting style. We now know that this is not so. In order to understand those findings, it is necessary to understand the distinction between two categories of potential environmental influences: shared versus non-shared features of the environment.

Shared features of the environment are those aspects of an individual's environment that are necessarily shared with other children in the family, contributing to similarities between family members. Some examples would be diet, geography, or social status, all considered as shared environment only if they contribute to greater similarity among individuals living in the same household. Modest shared environmental influences have been reported as being more significant during childhood and adolescence.

Non-shared features of the environment are any aspects of the environment and any experiences that can be different between children within the same family, contributing to differences between family members. Non-shared environment accounts for most environmental influence in psychopathology, personality, and cognitive abilities after adolescence. Some clear examples would be friendships or hobbies.

More generally, we can say that different individuals evoke different responses from others and actively choose different experiences and different kinds of environments for themselves. Therefore, our perception and interaction with the world is influenced by the personality traits inherited from our parents, but also strongly shaped by our environment.

However, the genetic or environmental influence is not unidirectional or deterministic at all. Only in extreme cases, such as having a severe genetic condition or growing up in a highly stressful and traumatic environment, can the weight they pull not be counter-balanced by will. But, even then, there will still be some room for improvement and training to overcome those handicaps. Once more, the power to decide to do so lies within us.

3.6. Experiences, Expectations & Memory

The way we perceive and interact with the world every second is not a clean slate free from filters, with only the objective truth and perception playing a role. Every single choice we make, no matter how small, is influenced by our memory, and is therefore a result of how well we recall our past experiences and the outcomes we expect our actions will produce.

For example, when we want to grab a glass full of water, we already know how much strength we should apply to lift the glass, based on the previous experiences kept in our memory, and our general knowledge of the world. Obviously, given the amount of tiny decisions we face at almost every instant, most of those processes happen without the need of our conscious awareness so that we can use our limited cognitive resources for more important, difficult, or relevant tasks. This allows us to interact with the world in a dynamic way, and be more efficient, since we don't need to calculate and guess the outcome of every situation we face.

Evaluating evidence (especially when it is complicated or unclear) requires a great deal of mental energy and our brains prefer to take shortcuts. As many evolutionary scientists have pointed out, our minds are unequipped to handle the modern world. For most of human history, people experienced very little new information during their lifetimes and decisions tended to be survival based. However, in the rapidly changing and information filled social media fuelled society that we live in, sometimes making cognitive shortcuts and jumping ahead to what's expected of our actions, can drive us to the wrong conclusions and to making the wrong decisions as a result. This sets toxic patterns of behaviour that get reinforced over and over in a circle.

Have you ever noticed how satisfactory it is to be right about something? *"You are right"*... the most useless and satisfying expression in the vocabulary of any language. Most of the time, it doesn't even matter what you are right about: it still feels damn good to be correct. Sometimes, we might fall in the trap of chasing that feeling beyond the acceptable limits of stubbornness or wellness.

This cognitive generalisation is called the confirmation bias. A confirmation bias is a type of cognitive bias that involves favouring information that confirms your previously existing beliefs or biases. Confirmation bias is our tendency to cherry-pick information that confirms our existing beliefs or ideas. It explains why two people with opposing views on a topic can see the same evidence and come away feeling validated by it.

For example, imagine that a person holds a belief that left-handed people are more creative than right-handed people. Whenever this person encounters a person that is both left-handed and creative, they place importance on this evidence that supports what they already believe. This individual might even seek proof that further backs up this belief while discounting examples that don't support the idea. Confirmation biases affect how we gather information, but they also influence how we interpret and recall information.

Confirmation bias is important because it may lead people to hold strongly to false beliefs or to give more weight to information that supports their beliefs than is warranted by the evidence. People may be overconfident in their beliefs because they have accumulated evidence to support them, when in reality much of the evidence refuting their beliefs was overlooked or ignored. These factors may lead to risky decision-making and lead people to overlook warning signs and other important information.

It is also important to understand how memories are biologically made to further comprehend how early the cognitive biases might set in, affecting the way we interpret the world, and to fit those *links* into the rest of the network.

A memory is the reactivation of a specific group of neurons, formed from persistent changes in the strength of connections between neurons. But what allows a specific combination of neurons to be reactivated over any other combination of neurons?

The answer is synaptic plasticity. This term describes the persistent changes in the strength of connections, called synapses, between brain cells. These connections can be made stronger or weaker depending on when and how often they have been activated in the past. Active connections tend to get stronger, whereas those that aren't used get weaker and can eventually disappear entirely.

From a structural point of view, the brain has three types of memory processes: sensory register, short-term and long-term memory. On the opposite scale, we have forgetting, with two main theories trying to explain why it happens: the decaying theory where, if a certain memory isn't repeated, it will eventually deteriorate; and the interference theory, where the new information received by the brain replaces old information (such as the inability to remember an old password after you have created a new one).

There are around 100 billion neurons in a normal human brain, capable to make around 100 trillion synapses or connections between them, some of them being for the purpose of memory. That is an overwhelming number, more than the number of stars in the Milky Way. As far as research can explain, a memory is formed by reinforcing a certain circuit of connections between a (small or large) number of neurons. The opposite process should be true for you to forget about something.

However, what if each neuron could dynamically and actively change their network of connections in order to make a memory, so that this single neuron could, in fact, be involved in the dynamic making of multiple memories? Then, instead of having one circuit that stays invariable for as long as you have that memory in storage, those same neurons could change their synapses and connect with others in order to bring to your consciousness a different memory.

By assuming this, the capacity of our brain to make and store memories (new or old) is virtually infinite. We would be able to remember something as long as the specific network of neurons is activated and interconnected. But, since this would involve thousands or millions of neurons, over time, when you recall the event again, maybe a handful of those neuronal networks would vary, making the event itself less and less accurate, and more and more influenced by our own cognitive biases, expectations and beliefs – remember, the motivation to be right is strong.

Considering all those cognitive challenges, how objective and helpful is a perception of the world that is being filtered by your consciousness? I guess what I am trying to say is that, despite the Quantum Psychology principle stating that you should always have conviction when following your gut instinct, you should always question everything within your reality, starting from your own self-awareness and consciousness. But to do this we need to understand what our consciousness is. We will tackle that in the next chapter. Before we do, let's get back to our initial question.

3.7 How Is the Way You Solve a Riddle Correlated With the Number of Times You Get Sick?

Hopefully, after everything we have covered, your initial perception of this question has been challenged and perhaps even shifted. In order to better understand the solution to the puzzling question, and since there could be as many answers as there are people in the world, let's test two of the most extreme cases possible: one of a dysfunctional person and one of a well-adjusted one.

In the case of the dysfunctional individual, when that person experiences high levels of stress when facing challenges, they tend to focus on the problem itself rather than on the solution. Blinded by their own stress and overwhelmed with confirmation bias, the person will experience a tunnelling of their vision, paying attention only to certain parts of a given problem. This approach, although adaptive in the case of a life-or-death type stressful situation, is not very useful for longer-term social or logical problems.

In addition, adopting this cognitive approach, the brain will respond accordingly by secreting the hormones and neurotransmitters corresponding to situations of anxiety; in other words, high levels of cortisol and low levels of DOSE neurotransmitters. Overtime, this response to challenges might become a set and automated pattern of behaviour. That would imply that, under those types of situations, every single neuron and cell of their body would receive a steady shot of those kinds of substances, and little or none of the positive ones.

In the longer term, when facing a general state of alarm or anxiety, the cognitive system, cells, and organs, will need fewer clues to label a situation as such and respond in that dysfunctional pattern of behaviour (remember, we always want to be right). Therefore, the repeated exposure to those levels of hormones and neurotransmitters will end up affecting the way every cell will code proteins, biased by the general state of stress, which will only serve to further reinforce the situation.

As a result, the epigenetic mechanisms of that person will reflect those overwhelming and dysfunctional reactions, making them more likely to be passed on to the next generation (especially if reinforced by the environment).

Finally, this persistent and stressful perception of reality will be assimilated as the natural state of mind, affecting the immune system, which is highly sensitive to our moods and feelings. Once your immune system is compromised, you will be more likely to get sick much more often. Therefore, the way you confront and face even the simplest of logical riddles will have an impact on how often you will get sick.

On the other hand, let's suppose the individual adopts a more adaptive mechanism in the face of challenges. That person will be more likely to focus on the solution when faced with a logical problem, being able to find creative and out-of-the-box responses. As this pattern expands and becomes a general response to the social environment, the person will also broaden their perception, creating fewer negative cognitive biases when assessing the behaviour of other people. As a result, every single cell, neuron and organ within their body will be getting a healthy amount of the DOSE hormones and neurotransmitters, and therefore, in the long term, coding proteins in a healthier way.

Finally, the epigenetic mechanisms that the person will pass on to the next generation (alongside environmental influence) will likely be much more adaptive and adjusted to thrive in the social world. In the longer term, the immune system will benefit from the lack of stress, making it more robust and resistant to illness, and therefore, less likely to get sick.

Does it make more sense now? Of course, this is a simplified example, and in reality the way our *links* interact is much more complex and difficult to measure or perceive. Furthermore, changing an assimilated pattern of behaviour can be one of the hardest things to do. However, at the very least, I hope the example shows the control we have over pretty much every aspect of our life, and how they are connected with one another.

Now we are almost ready to explore the extent to which Quantum Psychology allows us to expand the control that we have over our environment and reality. However, we didn't mention one of the main *links* involved in the process of understanding our true limits as beings, our (sub) conscious. Because, where does our (sub) conscious stand in this complex equation?

CHAPTER 4: UNVEILING OUR (SUB) CONSCIOUSNESS

We have now explored how different *links,* or aspects of our life, can be interconnected, and how the change in one of them can set off a chain reaction affecting other *links*. However, all of that, and all you are as a being, would not matter at all if we didn't consider the very factor that makes us aware of reality and of even being alive: consciousness.

The concept of consciousness is a tricky one. In many aspects, the term could be indistinctively interchanged with the social conception we have when referring to the soul or spirit. But consciousness is also that voice inside our mind, the one that tells us that we are alive, the very same thing that enables us to experience the world, interact with it, influence it, and vice versa.

Make no mistake; every single living animal, plant or even unicellular being has some level of consciousness. Even the smallest microscopic living being has the consciousness or the instinct to approximate or flee in response to stimuli in their environment. Consciousness, at whichever level it is experienced, is a fundamental requirement for life. Obviously, the degree of consciousness varies between species, between specimens of the same species, or even within the same living entity at different periods. So, what makes humankind so special and unique, consciousness-wise?

Unlike any of the known species on Earth, humans are able to appreciate qualitative and quantitative differences in the rest of the beings on Earth. We can think of consciousness as if it were a puzzle: human consciousness is a large and complex puzzle, with many pieces and colours, making it unique and more advanced than any other species. Nevertheless, every single living entity has its *consciousness puzzle*, just not quite as complicated as ours. Just as with DNA, the set of basic instructions shared by all living creatures, the complexity and distribution of the chromosomes varies between species, making all life so diverse and vibrant.

One problem in the study of consciousness is a lack of a universally accepted operational definition. The famous philosopher Descartes proposed the idea *"cogito, ergo sum"* (I think, therefore I am), suggesting that the very act of thinking demonstrates the reality of one's existence and consciousness. Today, consciousness is often viewed as an individual's awareness of their internal states, as well as the events going on around them. From this point of view, if you can describe something that you are experiencing in words, then it is part of your consciousness.

Consciousness is involved in everything you experience. It is in the tune stuck in your head, the sweetness of chocolate mousse, the throbbing pain of a toothache, and the bitter knowledge that eventually all feelings will end. Consciousness refers to your awareness of your unique thoughts, memories, feelings, sensations, and environment, differentiating you from other beings and objects. One of the most elegant definitions of consciousness is given by the philosopher Thomas Nagel, who said that *'consciousness is what it feels like'*.

Your conscious experiences are constantly shifting and changing. For example, at one moment you may be focused on reading this chapter. Then your consciousness may turn to the memory of a conversation you had with a co-worker. Next, you might notice how uncomfortable your chair is, or maybe you start mentally planning your dinner. This ever-shifting stream of thoughts can change dramatically from one moment to the next, but your experience of it seems smooth and effortless. Consciousness is occasionally confused with the conscience. It is important to note that while consciousness involves awareness of yourself and the world, your conscience is related to your morality, your sense of right and wrong.

Research on consciousness has focused on understanding the neuroscience behind our conscious experiences. Scientists have even utilised brain-scanning technology to seek out specific neurons that might be linked to different conscious events.

The quest to understand what consciousness is, and how it works, is filled with challenges and disagreements. In this regard, it is key to consider complex aspects of the topic such as: language and cultural differences, the various states of consciousness, the partitioning and layering of awareness, subjective experiential consciousness, awareness of the self, morality, and the problem of fitting the mind and behaviour into this equation, to name a few.

Furthermore, and adding to the previous issues (or overlapping some of them), we are not always fully aware of all the decisions we make, as we saw in the previous chapter. This is where the subconscious and the unconscious fit into this riddle. Sigmund Freud was probably the first to popularise ideas of the subconscious and unconscious minds in mainstream society. Although his theories have subsequently been widely disputed in psychology circles, as they are very difficult to prove, Freud created a useful model of the mind, which he separated into three tiers or sections – the conscious mind or ego, the preconscious, and the unconscious mind.

Freud's proposal has also been criticised because of its lack of elasticity in terms of what each level of consciousness involves, or the range of awareness we have (Freudians claim that no more than 10% of what happens in the mind reaches our consciousness). As is the case with many other attributes, individual differences, and training, are key to estimating the values and nature of the (sub) consciousness.

Nevertheless, it is true that there is a lot more to our consciousness than we are generally aware of. Henry

Ford said, *"Whether you think you can, or you think you can't, you're right!"* For years now, we have been hearing about the power of positive thinking. A question we might ask of those who make this statement is: where does this power come from, and how do we practically harness its potential to bring greater health and balance into our lives?

In 1963, Dr Joseph Murphy wrote a book called "The Power of Your Subconscious Mind". This classic self-help title explains that the power behind the thought is the subconscious mind. It turns out that it is the thoughts and beliefs held in the subconscious mind that create the bulk of the reality we experience. It is the subconscious that we need to pay attention to if we want to make rapid and lasting change in our lives and perception of reality. From this perspective, the conscious mind is volitional, it is the part of the mind that sets goals and judges the results. It can think abstractly and in terms of the past and the future, and is not limited to the present.

Coaching, self-help books, and other change processes, mostly focus on the conscious mind. These processes can be highly effective for some change, or a waste of energy if the subconscious mind is not aligned with the change. Because of this, training our subconscious awareness, and unveiling the full nature and potential of it, might be key to unfolding our real potential.

So why would the subconscious mind not be aligned with our conscious goals? The subconscious mind primarily develops between birth and the age of six or seven. During this time, it is a sponge, accepting whatever programming it receives from its environment in the form of experiences, attitudes, values and beliefs. Based on these experiences, and what might be told to us by our primary caregivers, we may take on such beliefs as "I will never be good enough", "I have to work hard to live", "No one will ever love me" or "I am always sick".

These belief programs will continue to run throughout our lives, giving us the conscious thoughts of "never good enough", "hard work for every dime", or the experience of rejection and ill health. If we have an experience as a child of falling out of a tree, we may "install" a phobia program that generalises to "all heights are dangerous". When we are "triggered", whether by our parents, partners, or strangers, and we immediately react in anger, sadness, self-condemnation, anxiety, etc., the "trigger" input is just like clicking an icon on a computer, starting a reactive program installed earlier in life. Because of these limiting belief programs running in our subconscious mind, we may sabotage our relationships, our health, our prosperity or our spiritual growth. As these toxic patterns of behaviour continue to run, they feed our thoughts and create a "printout" in our life experience, congruent with the underlying programs.

Now, let me tell you about the amazing neuroscience behind all these levels of the human mind. If I ask you, are you conscious right now? You'd go right ahead and tell me – yes. That's because your conscious mind is constructing awareness in you about everything around you. And underneath that operation of your conscious mind there are billions of neurons working in perfect harmony. Various brain regions work together to construct your conscious awareness of your environment. In this construction process there are two brain regions that require specific mention: the limbic system, and the frontal lobes of your brain, which are also directly connected with your raw emotions.

Emotions and behaviours that the prefrontal cortex deems as inappropriate never reach the surface of your conscious mind. They are trashed, sent into the depth of your subconscious mind, and remain hidden in your limbic system. This shows a direct channel and connection between our biological, social and physical reality, and the raw emotions that we experience, which connect us with those important to us. All of this is mediated and filtered by our (sub) consciousness.

Understanding the biology of consciousness (or self-awareness) is considered by some to be the final frontier of science. Over the last decade, a fledgling community of "consciousness scientists" have gathered some interesting information about the differences between conscious and unconscious brain activity. However, there is not yet any widely accepted theory that tackles the *what, why, where, how* and *when* of consciousness, or its value to us as individuals, or the universe as a reality that we live in. Previous attempts have used reductionist approaches for a matter as complex as consciousness, ignoring a central factor that is necessary to unravel the mystery.

Perhaps there is a part of our (sub) consciousness, where our true potential is hidden, that is governed by a set of laws different to those we know in the macroscopic world. What if a part of our (sub) consciousness could bend some of the biological limitations we experience, such as the flow of time and constriction of space?

71

Introducing the Quantum Realm

We have gone through quite a heavy chunk of widely studied theoretical and scientific concepts. Along the way, I have hinted at more mysterious concepts such us the Quantum Self, Quantum Psychology and the Quantum Realm. Where do these terms fit with our (sub) consciousness and the Chain Link Theory?

Although we will cover those topics in the upcoming chapters, I want to give you a little introduction by explaining how they fit in the theoretical frame of the Chain Link Theory. As mentioned before, consciousness gives sense to everything we know and experience, to the world around us. It is the glue that keeps everything that we experience as reality together, preventing it from falling apart. If we weren't conscious of the world and ourselves, we would be nothing but zombies with no purpose, and life, as we know it, would not exist.

But, as mentioned, even the concept of something as familiar to us as consciousness, is elusive and full of its own riddles. This happens because some part of it is easily experienced and understood from our own intuition, while another part (the subconscious) is mostly invisible to our awareness, despite its importance when interacting with our environment. For centuries scientists and philosophers have gone in circles trying to find the missing pieces to fully unveil what determines how the world is presented to us. Despite all the research on the subject, it still feels as if we are unable to see the whole picture of our reality. There is just too much that escapes our understanding and awareness, although we can naturally feel it there; there is something about our biological and social perception of the physical world that is limited and incomplete.

Quantum Psychology gives us that central piece, opening up the Quantum Realm and, with it, any hope of understanding our (sub) consciousness. By Quantum Realm I mean everything that belongs to and is ruled by the tricky and odd laws of the subatomic world (Quantum Mechanics). By understanding the concepts and the laws of the Quantum Realm from a wider perspective, we will acquire a deeper understanding of our own nature. With these tools, we are able to face the core of our essence as beings – our Quantum Self, the main energetic entity studied by Quantum Psychology.

It is now time to fully follow the white rabbit down the hole and challenge everything we have been led to believe.

CHAPTER 5: THE BASICS OF QUANTUM MECHANICS

Let's play a game. We all have imagined having a superpower. Most likely, you even have a list of your favourite superpowers, like unnaturally enhanced strength, time travel, invisibility, or being able to identify sour pistachios before eating them, for instance. Mine, by the way, would be the superpower of levitating and flying at a high speed.

But imagine, for a moment, that some sort of cosmic and superior force actually grants you a superpower: the capacity to perceive your life as if from the dimension of space-time, and to manipulate and perceive this dimension as easily as we manipulate the three spatial dimensions we already know and interact with.

Something like if you were able to "oversee" your whole life from above, every second of it, as a sequence of frames on a movie roll, ready to be projected at an old cinema. With this newly acquired skill, you could visualise every single instant of your entire life, frame by frame, instance by instance, sequence by sequence – past, present, and future. Then, imagine scrolling through your film backwards and forwards as you please, landing in the exact moment that you wish to live and experience all over again. Furthermore, you would be consciously aware of the implications that your "present" choices would have on your "future", as you would always be able to see what will happen next. This, my friend, would be the gift of mastering time.

But there is more to this cosmically gifted superpower. In each instance, as you are now able to view your whole life and move through all your experiences at will, you are also able to "sculpt" each one of the frames that form your entire life from beginning to end. Something like if you could use your hands to carve and change anything you wanted from those frames before landing into them: bringing people closer to you physically or emotionally, or distancing yourself from aspects and details that you find draining and counterproductive. Like getting your hands dirty while moulding clay, you would have the ability to mould each moment to the exact shape you desire. This, my friend, would be the gift of mastering space.

If you had that level of awareness and control over time and space, your consciousness would make you master of every event of your life. At the same time, you would alter everything and everyone around you, setting in motion events that would resonate like an explosive wave within your world. This force would eventually fade, like ripples from a pebble thrown into a lake. What would you do if you were the guardian of such immense powers? Lucky for us, there is no being in our physical reality with such a heavy burden of responsibility... or is there?

Believe it or not, there is a fundamental part of our existence and the Universe that somewhat masters those gifts. A set of scientific laws under which time and space are not absolute, nor chained to the linearity and immediacy of the macroscopic world that we biologically know. The science that studies this odd reality has been around for just over two hundred years, and experiments performed in this field consistently produce results that challenge everything we know about the world as we experience it. It shows that the way we are set by default to interact and survive in the world is not all there is to the picture, challenging everything we know about makes us "alive" and different from inanimate objects.. Of course, this science is called Quantum Mechanics or Quantum Physics.

If you already know the basics of Quantum Physics, then you know what type of mind-blowing experimental results I'm talking about. And the most amazing thing about this science is that if you think you understand the logic behind those results, it is because you don't have a clue about Quantum Mechanics; the more you learn about this science, the less you will feel you understand its meaning and implications... That is the enchanting paradox of this science.

If you are unfamiliar with the principles and properties of Quantum Physics, we are about to touch on some daunting and counter-intuitive concepts such as the double-slit experiment and its variations, Quantum Entanglement, or how time and space simply don't apply as we would expect at this subatomic level. But, above all, the lesson Quantum Physics teaches us is that the mere fact of having a conscious observer (that includes each one of us) changes the properties of subatomic particles – and therefore matter, and reality – as if they know we are observing them. This is known as the uncertainty principle.

On top of all that, Quantum Physics shows us that, when it comes to shaping and unveiling the reality we live in, our own (sub) consciousness is far more important than we give it credit for. For, in the Quantum Realm, time and space are at *our* disposal too. Our (sub) consciousness is the answer and the missing piece to explaining and connecting all those troublesome questions of life and reality; and is, ultimately, the key to unleashing our unique potential as human beings. Like the glue that holds everything together, or the orchestra conductor that directs and oversees everything else, our (sub) consciousness enables our sense of continuity and existence, which is needed for the Universe to exist. Ultimately, this leads us to Quantum Psychology and why it is important. But we will get there soon enough.

Before, let's go back a couple of steps and dig into understanding how the quantum reality works. Quantum Theory studies the principles, laws and "behaviours" of the smallest known particles: subatomic particles that compose and build the entire Universe (from matter, to light, to dark matter, to every single cell in your body).

Classical physics, or the physical laws based on the biological and physical world that we observe with our default sensory system, depicts nature at an ordinary (macroscopic) scale. Illustrated by Isaac Newton, it describes forces like gravity, or the trajectory of a football after you kick it. At this level, the laws are rigid, inherent within the assumptions of a linear and predictable time and space.

On the contrary, in quantum mechanics, the energy, momentum, angular momentum, and other quantities of a bound system are restricted to discrete values (quantisation), objects have characteristics of both particles and waves (wave-particle duality), and there are limits to the precision with which quantities can be measured (uncertainty principle), amongst other counter-intuitive properties. Quantum Mechanics gradually arose from observations from the subatomic world, which could not be reconciled with classical physics in the early 20th century. Long story short, what the evidence showed made no sense whatsoever to our intuition and perception of how reality works.

Whether you are ready or not, if this is your first contact with the Quantum Realm, your world is about to spin and turn upside-down as we depict some of the basic rules and principles of the subatomic world.

5.1. The Uncertainty Principle

The uncertainty principle, introduced by physicist Werner Heisenberg in 1927, is one of the most famous (and probably misunderstood) ideas in quantum physics. It shows a fuzziness in nature, a fundamental limit to what we can know about the behaviour of quantum particles and, therefore, the smallest known scale of nature. At these scales, the most we can hope for is to calculate the probabilities for where these particles are and how they will behave. Unlike Isaac Newton's clockwork macroscopic Universe, where everything follows clear-cut laws on how to move, where prediction is easy if you know the starting conditions, the uncertainty principle enshrines a level of fuzziness into quantum theory. That is, even if you "left" one of those subatomic particles at a given place and with a particular nature, when you next observe it, you cannot expect those values to have persisted, not like reality as we know it, where you can leave a dirty mug in the sink, and look again a second later to find it still there.

Wait, what? Exactly. When we talk about subatomic particles, you just cannot be certain about the time and space those particles can be found at. The uncertainty principle says that we cannot measure the position *and* the momentum of a particle with absolute precision. The more accurately we know one of these values, the less accurately we know the other.

This is what Niels Bohr proposed with the Copenhagen interpretation of Quantum Theory, which asserts that a particle is whatever it is measured to be (for example, a wave or a particle), but that it cannot be assumed to have specific properties, or even to exist, until it is measured. In short, Bohr was saying that objective reality does not exist. This translates to a principle called superposition, which claims that as long as we do not know what the state of any object is, it is actually in all possible states simultaneously, until we look to check.

To illustrate this theory, we can use the famous and somewhat macabre analogy of Schrodinger's Cat. First, we have a living cat and place it in a thick lead box. At this stage, there is no question that the cat is alive. We then throw in a vial of cyanide and seal the box. We do not know if the cat is alive or if the cyanide capsule has broken and the cat has died. Since we do not know, in the Quantum Realm the cat is both dead and alive – in a superposition of states. It is only when we break open the box and see the condition of the cat that the superposition is lost, and the cat must be either alive or dead. This, unthinkable in our experience of reality, is what is constantly happening at a subatomic scale.

One way to think about the uncertainty principle is as an extension of how we see and measure things in the everyday world. You can read these words because particles of light, photons, have bounced off the screen or paper and reached your eyes. Each photon on that path carries with it some information about the surface it has bounced from, at the speed of light.

However, when you try to do this with a subatomic particle, such as an electron, it is not so simple. You might similarly bounce a photon off it and then hope to detect that photon with an instrument. But chances are that the photon will impart some momentum to the electron as it hits it, changing the path of the particle you are trying to measure. Or else, given that quantum particles often move so fast, the electron may no longer be in the place it was when the photon originally bounced off it. Either way, your observation of either position or momentum of either particle will be inaccurate and, more importantly, the act of observation affects the particle being observed.

Yes, you read that right: the act of your conscious observation affects the way the particle being observed is going to behave. But, how can the particle know you are observing it, right? That same question puzzled Einstein for decades.

Here's a taste of that weirdness: If you hit a baseball over a pond, it sails through the air to land on the other shore. If you drop a baseball in a pond, waves ripple away in growing circles. Those waves eventually reach the other side. In both cases, something travels from one place to another. But the baseball and the waves move differently. A baseball doesn't ripple or form peaks and valleys as it travels from one place to the next. Waves do. In experiments, particles in the subatomic world sometimes travel like waves. And they sometimes travel like particles. Why the tiniest laws of nature work that way isn't clear – to anyone.

But, how is all this apparently and intuitive non-sense even possible? Let's talk about one of the most well-known experiments in the field of Quantum Mechanics.

5.2. The Double Slit Experiment

The double slit experiment was designed by Thomas Young in 1801, over one hundred years before Quantum Mechanics even became a real thing. It is, in my opinion, one of the most elegant and neat paradigms ever designed in any science, because of its simplicity, sturdiness and replicability. The double-slit experiment is a demonstration that light and matter can display characteristics of both classically defined waves and particles.

Imagine an experimental setup where a machine gun sprays paint bullets at a screen in which there are two narrow and parallel vertical openings, or slits, with another screen (this one without slits) situated behind it. As you start to fire the paint gun, three things can happen: the bullets can collide with the first screen without going through either of the slits; the bullets can go through the slit on the right; or the bullets can go through the slit on the left. Considering the last two options: as we fire hundreds of bullets, eventually we will get a pattern on the second screen consisting of two parallel and vertical colourful lines, corresponding to each one of the slits through which the bullets have passed.

Easy, right? Now, let's repeat the experiment firing light beams, subatomic particles in the form of photons, instead of paint bullets. Intuition would argue that we should expect a similar resulting pattern on the second screen as we did before. However, when Young ran this experiment, he found that the pattern drawn on the second screen by the subatomic particles consisted of a series of parallel lines spread across all the screen, instead of only two, as would be expected.

This result, which can seem odd, meant that the particles were behaving as waves instead of as "solid matter". To understand it, imagine that, instead of solid bullets or atoms, we pushed a wave of water towards this double slit screen. As you can probably intuit, once the water goes through each slit simultaneously, it will collide right behind the first screen, expanding parallel and smaller waves until all those waves reach the second screen, forming a pattern of parallel lines on said screen. Makes sense, right? The only thing is that single subatomic particles were fired at the screen, and somehow still produced the wave pattern, as if they had somehow managed to go through both slits at the same time.

Therefore, light behaved as a wave, emerging from both slits and interfering each other. If their peaks coincide, they reinforce each other, whereas if a peak and a trough coincide, they cancel out. This wave interference is called diffraction, and it produces the parallel patterns on the back screen, where the light waves are either reinforced or cancelled out.

But how the hell could a single particle be in two places at the same time?? This is exactly what Young and his team wondered two hundred odd years ago. The team then decided to directly "observe" the first screen in order to see how the single particle could "split" itself and go through both slits at the same time. However, after firing thousands of a given subatomic particle, when they then looked at the pattern formed in the second screen, there were only two bigger parallel lines right behind each one of the slits, just as it would happen with the paint bullets. What had happened is that each particle then behaved as intuitively expected by going through only one of the slits, acting as solid matter and not as a wave. Therefore, the way atoms behaved actually changed, depending on whether someone was observing them or not.

Wait, hold on a second... WHAT THE HECK? Exactly. Somehow subatomic particles "know" and are affected by our own perception or awareness of them.

Yet a third experiment variation was performed. This time, the "observer" was located halfway between the first and the second screen, in order to try to capture the moment when the atoms would split themselves to behave as waves. If you are not yet dizzy, sit down as it gets even weirder: in this instance, despite the first observation detecting that the atoms were going through both slits and acting as a wave, as soon as they "hit" the level where the observer was waiting for them, they "went back in time" and were "forced" to choose only one of the slits to go through. Therefore, even if they started as a wave, they would retrace their steps and pass through only one of the slits to behave as a solid particle and create the pattern consisting of two parallel lines in the second screen.

Take a few seconds to let this all sink in...

Before you let your scepticism kick your intellectual ego (I certainly did the first time I learnt about the double-slit experiment), bear in mind that this is one of the most replicated experiments in the history of science. And the results have always been the same, without exception. In fact, the predictions (or technically the lack of them) that you can make in Quantum Mechanics are even more reliable than the ones you can make in the "real" world of macroscopic physics that we interact with. The way the subatomic world behaves is even more reliable than assuming the sun will rise in the east tomorrow.

But how does this affect you as an individual and the world we all live in? Well, for a start, everything in this Universe is made of those subatomic particles that decide that time and space is something that will not stop them from doing as they please. Additionally, the fact that our mere observation determines the way those particles behave, creating our reality, shows the importance that each one of us, as conscious individuals, has in determining the way the Universe is set up.

However, we haven't finished exploring the weirdness of the subatomic world yet. Sit and enjoy.

5.3. Entanglement

There is a concept in Quantum Physics that holds that subatomic particles can be linked, even if they are not physically near one another, this is called Quantum Entanglement. This principle shows that subatomic particles can link their properties with one another at great distances – perhaps at opposite ends of the universe.

When two quantum objects interact in the right way, the information they contain becomes shared. This can result in a kind of connection between those particles, where an action performed on one will automatically affect the nature of the other. For example, if we make one atom spin clockwise, the entangled particle will start to spin counter clockwise, even if we don't perform any action on it. This unbreakable entanglement applies even if the two particles very far apart. And this will happen instantaneously, even faster than the speed of light – which is meant to be the speed limit of the universe.

To further understand what entanglement implies, imagine that you and a friend had two entangled coins. You each take your coins home and then flip them at the same time. If yours comes up heads, then at the exact same moment you know your friend's coin has just come up tails, breaking all the space and time limitations we know.

The concept of entanglement found a very powerful sceptic in the 1920s: Albert Einstein. For Einstein, the "spooky action at distance" (his description of entanglement), just couldn't be possible. He claimed that he couldn't believe that God would play dices with nature, as those results from the subatomic world, implying that information were moving faster than the speed of light, contradicted some of his predictions formulated in the Relativity Theory. However, over the following decades, it was widely proved that this was one of the very few scientific findings were Einstein was wrong.

How do the principles of entanglement, no matter how odd and counter-intuitive they seem, affect our daily life and perception? Well, for now let's just say that we are ultimately made of the same particles capable of bending the rules of time, space and connection that we are accustomed to. Furthermore, as we covered before, those particles bow to our conscious observation. Of course, there is still more we can learn about reality by playing with atoms.

5.4. Teleportation

Humankind has been fantasising about teleportation for a long time. Sci-fi movies like Star Trek play with our imagination and the possibility of going from point A to point B, no matter how far apart they are, instantly. Imagine the incredible advantages, if only it were possible. Well, when we talk about subatomic particles and the laws of Quantum Mechanics, teleportation also becomes a reality, challenging our assumptions about the universe.

To test the possibility of teleporting particles, an experiment was performed some years ago in La Palma and Tenerife, islands in the Canary Islands archipelago. The research team successfully connected a quantum teleportation system that set a new distance record for the spooky communications technique. The scientific team in La Palma generated an entangled pair of photons (A and B, for instance), and then sent photon A over a non-quantum channel (a fibre) to Tenerife. The teleportation photon (let's call it C), which was generated by a third

92

party in La Palma, was provided to the lab were photon B was located, and when photon C's state was projected onto photon B, photon A was able to measure its state at the far end of the link, a whole 143kms away. Therefore, the information from photon C was sent directly to photon A, even though they never interacted or exchanged information directly, through photon B and its entanglement to photons A.

But would it be possible to replicate the basics of the experiment at a macroscopic level? Allowing us to project an identical subatomic set-up thousand, or even millions, of kilometres away? Teleportation would mean combining trillions of atoms, in exactly the same way they are formed in our bodies right now, but in a different place. If it were possible, our body, cells and atoms, would disappear and cease to exist in point A, and would be reconfigured identically in point B, no matter how far.

But, if we got rid of our body and every particle of it, would we still be the same person, even if every single atom within us was set up exactly the same way somewhere else? Let's continue testing the limits and flexibility of reality.

5.5. Quantum Tunnelling

Quantum Tunnelling is the quantum mechanical phenomenon whereby a particle passes through a potential barrier that, according to classical mechanics, it cannot surmount. Like if you could go through a solid wall without breaking or affecting the nature of the wall. The barrier can be a physically impassable medium, like an insulator or a vacuum, or it can be a region of high potential energy.

This plays an essential role in several physical phenomena, such as the nuclear fusion that occurs in stars like the Sun. It has important applications to modern devices such as quantum computing, and the scanning tunnelling microscope, an instrument, which can create images of surfaces at the atomic level.

Tunnelling is often explained in terms of the uncertainty principle that we saw earlier, where, in the general case, the quantum object has more than one fixed state (not a wave nor a particle). Due to the wave-like property of particles, Quantum Physics predicts that there is a finite probability that an object trapped behind a barrier (without the energy to overcome the barrier) may at times appear on the other side of the barrier, without actually overcoming it or breaking it down. For instance, if an electron approaches an electric field and is repelled by it, there is nevertheless some probability, however small, that it will find itself on the other side of the field.

It can perhaps be best visualised by imagining a broad wave approaching and then slightly overlapping a barrier. Although the main part of the wave may never penetrate the barrier, a small part of it does, allowing for the possibility of the particle that is generating the wave suddenly being located on the other side of the barrier.

In classical mechanics, if a particle has insufficient energy to overcome a potential barrier, it simply won't. In the quantum world, however, particles can often behave like waves. On encountering a barrier, a quantum wave will not end abruptly – its amplitude will decrease exponentially. This drop in amplitude corresponds to a drop in probability of finding a particle, as you look further into the barrier. If the barrier is thin enough, the amplitude may be non-zero on the other side, so, there is a finite probability that some of the particles will tunnel through the barrier.

Once again, the subatomic world, with which we interact and are part of to the last cell of our organism, shows us that the way we perceive time and space as fixed entities might not be accurate. However, as the Quantum Realm is based in probabilities and not in certainties, what if there are parallel realities for each one of those possible outcomes?

5.6. Multiverse Theory

The Multiverse Theory suggests the idea that our universe may be one of many (perhaps an infinite number) of alternative universes and that different things may simultaneously happen in each. Therefore, technically everything possible and conceivable might be happening in a parallel universe. But, how would that even be possible?

The multiverse theory holds that, as soon as a potential exists for any object to be in any state, the universe of that object transmutes into a series of parallel universes equal to the number of possible states in which that object can exist, with each universe containing a unique single possible state of that object. Furthermore, there is a mechanism for interaction between these universes that somehow permits all states to be accessible in some way and for all possible states to be affected in some manner.

Anthony Leggett has been thinking about this paradox for fifty years. He is a physicist at the University of Illinois at Urbana-Champaign and winner of the 2003 Nobel Prize for physics. Leggett sees two ways to explain the problem of the Schrödinger's cat paradigm. One way is to assume that quantum theory will eventually fail in some experiments, although there is no evidence supporting this will happen. The other possibility implies that, as scientists conduct quantum experiments on larger groups of particles, the theory will hold. And those experiments will unveil new aspects of Quantum Theory. Eventually, they will be able to see more of the whole picture, including realizing that our world is one of many. If true, then in the thought experiment, Schrödinger's cat would be alive in half the worlds – and dead in the rest.

If the many-world idea is true, then a particle might be in one place in this world, and somewhere else in other worlds, as we have previously seen. This morning, you probably chose which shirt to wear and what to eat for breakfast. But according to the *many worlds* idea, there is another world where you made different choices.

The idea of infinite parallel universes co-existing beyond our awareness is a bold and interesting concept. However, given the amount of tiny decisions that every single living being is constantly making (not only on Earth, but in the whole Universe), if every one of those countless decisions opened the door to further multi-verses, the result would be very complicated and chaotic.

Furthermore, although the multiverse theory is something physicists have been theorising for decades now, no firm conclusion has been reached. Just as with Quantum Mechanics in general, it appears as though every time scientists look out into the universe or through a subatomic microscope, they just find more riddles and questions than answers; they find descriptive science and not predictive science.

What if we reversed the approach and started looking within ourselves, instead of to the outside world to find the explanation for our existence?

5.7. Conclusions

Throughout this chapter we have briefly walked through some of the most basic principles and experiments within Quantum Physics. If this was your first contact with this science, you may be feeling a bit overwhelmed by all the information, conclusions and implications presented (I certainly did for some days when I discovered it). However, you have probably also noticed that all the evidence shown, although highly interesting and mind-challenging, lacks practical applications in our daily life: basically it is a lot of descriptive stuff, belonging to the subatomic world, and difficult to extrapolate to the macroscopic reality we live in.

This is exactly what Physics has been struggling with when it comes to the quantum world: there is some sort of "gap" or jump from how subatomic particles interact with reality, compared to how we do. Up until now, there has not been any plausible explanation to connect both worlds and the laws governing them. There is no "quantum bridge" that can bring those cool space-time superpowers from the world of particles into ours.

Quantum Mechanics has brought important advances and applications into our world (lasers, computing, automation...), although it seems as if we have merely scratched the surface of its potential. To access its full potential we need to understand and fully embrace the way the Quantum Realm works. Were we to find the connection between the quantum and the macroscopic reality, we could benefit from all the rule-bending principles of the subatomic world. But how can we break the barrier of space and time that limits our biological existence?

Not to get ahead of ourselves though, but this is exactly what Quantum Psychology brings to our understanding of ourselves and the universe; allowing us to become that bridge that connects quantum and macroscopic physics, and thus affecting our daily life and the way reality unfolds for us.

Perhaps we do possess some of the superpowers we were talking about at the beginning of the chapter; we are just not conscious of our own potential, and therefore unable to unleash it... Perhaps, instead of trying to find the answers outside, we should look within ourselves. After all, we had all the required clues all along: the uncertainty principle, entanglement, tunnelling, teleportation... And specially the way our own conscious observation affects the results in the double-slit experiment.

Perhaps, the missing key to building the bridge and understanding the whole spectrum of quantum reality was right in front of us all along, within our (sub) consciousness.

It is now time to understand what Quantum Psychology is and implies.

CHAPTER 6: QUANTUM PSYCHOLOGY: DEFINITION AND IMPLICATIONS

It may now be clearer to you that we are not fully aware of our most basic and profound quality as beings, of the very thing that would help us understanding ourselves, and the Universe. Our perception of reality is restrained by our biological limitations, but maybe our consciousness doesn't have to be. Quantum Psychology challenges the way we perceive and interact with the world and what we call "reality".

Ok, after digging into some of the basic concepts that shape physical reality, it's time to unfold the bridge that connects everything else within the realm of our perceived, and deceiving, existence. This chapter will define Quantum Psychology and explain some of the most immediate implications drawn from it. Quantum Psychology is:

"The science and theory that studies the nature, implications, and relationships, between the part of our (sub) consciousness (or Quantum Self) governed by the laws of Quantum Mechanics, and how it retro-influences and interacts with our default sensory, cognitive, neuronal, social and biological mechanisms, including the rest of our (sub) consciousness, which are ruled by the macroscopic or Newtonian physical laws and limited by our biological and social experience of reality."

Fair enough, but what exactly does this definition imply for our daily life, right? For a start, and as we have previously covered, it is the nature of the subatomic or Quantum Realm that time and space are not linear. From a Quantum Psychology perspective, this allows us, through this part of our (sub) consciousness, to be aware of, and make decisions, based on "what goes on" in that Quantum plane. And what goes on is that our mind, or energetic field, interacts with the subatomic particles that move through us and form the entire Universe. Furthermore, when this contact is established, time and space are no longer subject to the same Newtonian linearity as the rest of our senses are. This opens a brand-new scope of possibilities and ways to thrive and reach our full potential.

Because of our biological nature and the adaptive configuration given by natural selection in order to survive, we are designed to experience time and space linearly and tied to the immediate perception of our environment, our experience, and our expectations. As a result, most of our Quantum interactions happen at a more instinctive and subconscious level, before (and if), it reaches conscious status. Even then, like with most of our conscious conclusions, we are often not fully aware of the true source of such conclusions, attributing them, instead, to different known phenomena. Furthermore, those final conclusions are integrated and formed by the rest of our sensory, cognitive, and biological systems.

Once you become aware of that part of your inherent nature – your Quantum Self – you will realise that you naturally have those superpowers which allow you to influence the arrangement of time and space, and how they unfolded to you, a skill that can be magnified and trained through self-awareness. Once you accept the effects that a conscious mind has over matter in the subatomic world (like in the double slit experiment), there is no way back to perceiving the world as you did before.

Pulling this thread unravels all of the questions of our existence and, eventually, to apprehending the implications of answering some of the biggest questions there are: what happens after death, the concept of God, time travelling, the meaning of life, teleportation, the origin of the Universe, and other previously unanswerable questions. And each one of these topics leads to one overwhelming conclusion: pretty much everything we experience, interact with, or perceive, is interconnected and retro-influenced one way or another. It's a continuous energetic exchange between individual beings, the world, and all living entities in the Universe (composed of the same basic ingredients as us).

The primary goal of Quantum Psychology is to study how that part of our (sub) consciousness (or Quantum Self) acts as a bridge between macroscopic and quantum physics. And, once this relationship is understood, draw on the implications and applications to reach our greatest potential. Imagine you could maximise the tangible impact you have on reality to influence any important aspect or goal in your life. Imagine you could train your awareness and perception to gather insights from different sections of time or space that go way beyond the limitations of your default sensory system. Imagine, from a social and technological point of view, the potential implications of discovering how, through the innate power of your mind, you can consciously influence matter and reality at a subatomic level. If we did have a way to measure and exploit this potential, where do you think the limit within each one of us would be set?

The essence of Quantum Psychology is that it hands the full power and responsibility of our own development to ourselves: no overwhelming divine force, no blaming on external or interpersonal factors, only the whole world in front of you to be perceived and conquered. We will always face situations that somewhat escape our control, or extreme events that overwhelm and challenge everything we believe in. Pain is inevitable; and what's more important, pain is an indivisible part of growing, self-development, and achievement.

But, even during those uncontrollable and painful times you still hold an inherent power and control: to decide how you react, and to shape and influence the message you are transmitting to the world through your response. Because, depending on that message, the final outcome of those situations will vary enormously. And, as mentioned before, subatomic particles don't bend to the rules of our biological time and space limitations.

In interaction with the rest of the *links*, the message we send out will interact with the rest of the Universe, before coming back to us. Like an echo, the returned message will partly reflect the very same thing we communicated – whether that message is based on an adjusted or dysfunctional response is, therefore, critical.

Does that mean that if we think positively all our problems will just vanish? Absolutely, and energetically, NO. First of all, we would need to frame how we define a problem; as, for some people, an event can be perceived as a problem if they feel they lost control over the outcome; however, for others, that same situation can be interpreted as an opportunity, if they decide to take it as a chance to grow and look within for self-development. If you choose the latter option, then you are setting up your system to find solutions: starting in the brain with the hormones and neurotransmitters produced, all the way to how you cognitively perceive and interpret every single social interaction you have.

In addition to this, you will also transmit and look for answers to the problem at a quantum level. At a subatomic level, all conceivable solutions to the problem (either positive, neutral or negative) exist simultaneously. Here, your Quantum Self and mind-set will play a role, influencing which one of those plausible outcomes will be more likely to materialise, based on the message you are sending. Because, being right is one of the strongest psychological principles of life.

Does this mean that if I want to win the lottery, all I have to do is to strongly think about it until my Quantum Self bounces me back the winning numbers from the future? Absolutely NOT. When we talk about the subatomic laws we can only talk about probabilities and possibilities, not about certainties. Even more, that would directly conflict and violate the forces of the macroscopic physics. Therefore, following the example of the lottery numbers, from a quantum perspective, absolutely all the possible combinations are happening at the same time. It's only when the present catches up, and those possible outcomes are forced into certainty, that one of them becomes what we understand to be real.

However, there is always a way around to maximise our chances of achieving a goal (i.e. which lottery number combination will win tonight): like finding patterns amongst the winning combinations, or coming up with systems that will make winning more likely, or simply finding other ways to achieve whatever it is that you are looking to accomplish by winning the lottery. And, one of the factors involved (alongside your cognitive thinking, IQ, access to resources, lack of physical or environmental handicaps...) will be your Quantum Self and how Quantum Psychology works from and through you.

The degree of complexity increases when other people also influence the particular outcome. Despite the fact that, from a quantum perspective we always have a degree of control over any outcome in our lives, when you include other people in the equation, their Quantum Selves also influence the outcome. Then, the prediction and full awareness of the situation usually becomes more difficult to isolate, train, and enhance, by an individual. Just like the skills, resources, and time required to learn how to ride a bike are not the same, or even accessible, compared with learning to pilot a plane or space rocket.

So, what part of your reality is due to Quantum Psychology? Above all, we find cues and experience Quantum Psychology through connecting with others in a meaningful way. The easiest and most instinctive way to perceive its effects is in little details that most of us have experienced during our lives. For example, when we are very close to someone, and we suddenly have the feeling that something is going on with that person, and then we make contact with them we realise that something has changed in their lives. Or when someone that we haven't met in a while comes to our mind and that very same day we bump into them in the middle of the street. Or when we dream about something happening and it does; or, at a deeper and more complex level, when we just know in our hearts that we have to do something regardless of the consequences, knowing that eventually we will find sense to the whole venture.

I know, I know. You might be thinking: what about all the times when we experience those situations, but they weren't real? Isn't what I'm proposing a clear case of confirmation bias? Perhaps some of the times we experience these kinds of situations and they don't materialise we are just experiencing cognitive bias. Perhaps, for the situations where what we felt actually ended up happening, we were still either following that bias or truly connected with the Quantum Realm through our Quantum Self. Perhaps, for the rest of the situations, we connect with the Quantum Realm, hinting at one of the possible outcomes to that specific situation, yet that wasn't the one materialised in the end. In other words: if you were tricked by an optical illusion, would you then claim that absolutely everything perceived by your eyes is inaccurate and misleading? Or would you try to discern the difference between 'what's real and what's not'?

Remember, there are no certainties in the Quantum world, only possibilities. And if we dream about something happening or think about someone we haven't met in a while, you can still not be certain that it will actually happen. In any case, you might be experiencing a hint from your Quantum Self, making you aware that this is one of the outcomes that has manifested in a reality of simultaneous possibilities. Then, between where you are and what actually happens when the moment comes, there is a path filled with countless decisions, made by you and all other beings, which will also interfere and influence the final materialisation. However, if you were able to train your sensitivity towards perceiving those signals, if you were able to heighten your awareness, at the very least you could use that information to do everything within your power to either maximise or minimise the chances of that event happening.

This view of reality implies that a part of our (sub) consciousness is actually ruled by Quantum Theory laws, not the macroscopic ones we are accustomed to. In this view, time or space are bent and, to a greater or lesser degree, shaped by the interpersonal connections that we make. This is the equivalent of Interpersonal Quantum Entanglement, energetic exchanges and connections with the beings with whom we are truly close. Because, there is yet another key point in Quantum Psychology: if our Quantum Self and (sub) consciousness sits at the centre of how reality and the Universe is formed and displayed (as claimed by Biocentrism, which we will cover in a later chapter) , at the centre of that centre, you will find that the real, raw, emotional and energetic connections that we make throughout our life are both the fuel and engine of our experiences, and our existence.

As with entangled particles, this allows us to experience and anticipate things about the people we are deeply connected to, beyond the linear reality of space and time. This would mean having additional, and invaluable, insights into some of the most important decisions we will ever make in life; even if they don't initially make sense to our conscious and present state of mind, limited as it is by our biological perception, memory, or expectations. When we follow the quantum trail that part of our (sub) consciousness hints us to, the ultimate meaning will eventually become apparent.

All you need to do is to be brave enough to follow your heart and instincts. Your Quantum Self might know things about you, and what's coming your way, before the rest of your consciousness does. And, if you are tuned and balanced with your physical and energetic environment, you will increase the number of those hints or hunches that whisper to you what you should do next. It is all about balance and self-awareness.

The secret to fully exploiting the potential of Quantum Psychology comes from balancing it with the rest of your *links* as well. Only when you follow your instinct, follow a healthy diet and lifestyle, and master the cognitive strategies required to interact with your environment in an adjusted way, can you exploit the benefits of having a part of your (sub) consciousness working for you at a quantum level. It only requires a dysfunction in one of those *links* to set a reaction and a pattern in motion that will intoxicate the rest of the network at different levels. However, it is extremely rare to find anyone for whom all links work in perfect balance. Therefore, it is about the forces, counter forces, and the weight of influences, on the final outcome in this ever-changing complex system.

Quantum Psychology is about realising that you can use the different rules set in Quantum Physics to your advantage to reach whatever you set yourself to. It's about giving you the ultimate power and responsibility over your own self-development and consciously training this part of your nature. It is also, at a wider level, about opening new doors for social and technological development that will take our species to a whole new level and change the world, as we know it.

Led by natural selection and our biological instincts, we have been slaves of our own immediate sensory and perceptual limitations. Because there is this part of your reality that is not limited by the now and here; from where you can take information about the possibilities of the future, or from other spatial locations, that can help you optimise your decision making here and now. The compass to navigate all that lie in the interpersonal connections and raw sensations that we live every moment.

Quantum Psychology is not exclusive to humankind at all. In fact, every single living organism in the Universe possesses some degree of connection with the Quantum Realm, as this energy is the basic ingredient that enables life itself. However, the range of awareness or retro-influence will vary in qualitative and quantitative terms from species to species, and even from specimen to specimen, or within the same specimen over time.

Quantum Psychology provides the central piece to the very complex riddle of how the Universe is made and how we influence and fit into it. It opens the door to new questions that need to be tackled, and its answers will resonate across other subjects. Because, make no mistake: Quantum Psychology is the most important piece of this puzzle, the one that will enable us to jump to a new era as a species and as beings, and also the one we are ignoring.

When we fully understand, measure, and control the potential of Quantum Psychology, we will be able to understand our own nature and the Universe itself; to find new ways to communicate with it and between ourselves; to reach new heights from a personal development and technological point of view; and tune all the *links* towards achieving our own personal goals, as we are indeed the main point of control for the final outcome.

The path to understanding the potential of Quantum Psychology is within you. So, if you want to hear it whispering to your consciousness, simply begin by listening to the silence of your own mind: by shutting down all the sources of distraction or stimuli that come from the sensory system that you have used and taken for granted your entire life. Just look within yourself and mentally observe how your gut feelings or raw sensations affect the way you make decisions in your daily life. Pay attention to those signs, the ones where you are conscious and aware of something that you know the classical physical laws cannot explain.

The story of Quantum Psychology is one about time, space, and profound interpersonal connections, and how those three terms, that we take for granted, can be misleading, even when their true nature is exposed before us. The clues leading to the unveiling of our Quantum Self come from very different perspectives, theories and sciences, as we will see in the upcoming chapters.

CHAPTER 7: THE (PSEUDO) SCIENTIFIC TRAIL TOWARDS QUANTUM PSYCHOLOGY

We have unveiled the definition of Quantum Psychology and its scientific backbone (Quantum Mechanics), alongside briefly depicting some of its implications. However, what other phenomena do we know that support the principles of Quantum Psychology? In the next two chapters we will explore experiments, experienced phenomena, theories, and examples that hint at the plausibility and potential hidden within our Quantum Self.

I will not claim that these perspectives represent irrefutable truth at all; in fact, quite the opposite, as most of them have been heavily questioned from different angles. However, each one of the upcoming approaches point towards how Quantum Psychology is inherent in each one of us, holding the key of awareness that will take us towards new levels of achievement. Each one of the ideas covered can't fully explain the whole picture, yet key concepts can be drawn from them to build that blurry and counter-intuitive puzzle of our true essence.

Furthermore, complex concepts, such as those covered by Quantum Psychology, can only be comprehended by adopting a holistic approach that combines perspectives of a very variable nature. The Buddhist parable about the blind men and the elephant illustrates this point beautifully. In this story a group of blind men hear that a strange animal called an elephant has been brought to the town, but none of them are aware of its shape or form. Out of curiosity, they say: "We must inspect and know it by touch, of which we are capable". So, they seek it out, and when they find it they grope about it. The first person, whose hand landed on the trunk says, "This being is like a thick snake". For another one, whose hand reaches its ear, it seems like a kind of fan. For another, whose hand is upon its leg, the elephant is a pillar, like a tree-trunk. The blind man who places his hand upon its side says the elephant "is a wall". Another, who felt its tail, describes it as a rope. The last felt its tusk, stating the elephant is that which is hard, smooth and like a spear.

Do you think any of the blind men truly understood the form and concept of what an elephant is? And, at the same time, weren't all of them also right in their description of the animal? The problem the blind men encountered in trying to comprehend the task they had, was one of perspective and interpretation: although all of them were right in their point of views, they were incomplete and reductionist in gathering the whole picture of what an elephant is.

Similarly, we will be exploring Quantum Psychology by presenting evidence that comes from different angles, sciences and even philosophies. Nevertheless, all of them will have something in common: describing an entity, bigger than we are, and inherent in the core of our own nature, which hints that there is a potential within that surpasses the biological limitations of time, space, and connection, as we know them. Or, at the very least, I hope those this body of ideas will wake up your curiosity to question some conventionalisms about reality.

7.1. The Experiments with Water Particles of Dr Masaru Emoto

Masaru Emoto (1943-2014) was a Japanese author and entrepreneur who claimed that human consciousness has an effect on the molecular structure of water. Dr Emoto revolutionised the idea that our thoughts and intentions affect the physical realm. For over 20 years, he studied the evidence of how the molecular structure in water transforms when it is exposed to human words, thoughts, sounds, and intentions.

For his research, Dr Emoto used Magnetic Resonance Analysis technology and high-speed photographs, separating water into 100 petri dishes and assigned each dish a fate: good or bad. The 'good' water was blessed or praised for being so wonderful, while the 'bad' water was scolded, then froze the water and examined the frozen crystals under a microscope. Dr Emoto claimed that positive words and emotions, classical music and positive prayer directed at the water produced beautiful crystals, while negative words and emotions and crude music, such as heavy metal, produced ugly crystals.

Some of the experiment variations showed that simply writing negative words on a container of water was enough to change the physical properties of that water. If such a claim were true it would require a fundamental change in our understanding of the basic forces of nature and how reality unfolds. His research also showed that polluted and toxic water, which he claims has deformed and chaotic, when exposed to prayer and positive intention, could be altered and restored to beautifully formed geometric crystals found in clean, healthy water.

In one experiment Dr Emoto had a team of about 2,000 people in Tokyo focus their thoughts on some water across the world in California, in a double-blind study. There was also another group of water samples, set aside in a different location used as controls, but the group was unaware of this fact. Ice crystals from both sets of samples were then identified and photographed by an analyst, and the images obtained were blindly assessed and critiqued for aesthetic appeal by 100 judges. Results, published in The Journal of Science and Healing (2006) indicated that *"crystals from the treated water were given higher scores for aesthetic appeal than those from the control water"*. According to these findings it would seem that through our consciousness we can directly alter the geometric shape and structure of water.

In another variation of the paradigm, Dr Emoto studied the effects on a bottle filled with raw rice and water. After thirty days, the bottle with a positive word on it began to ferment, giving off a strong, pleasant aroma. Contrarily, the bottle with the negative wording attached turned mostly black, and the control rice began to rot, turning a green-blue colour. However, according to Dr Emoto, it was the ignored rice that fared the worst.

Nevertheless, his work has been heavily criticised and challenged. One of the main points of scepticism comes from Dr Emoto revealing little about his exact procedures to obtain the photographs of the water crystals, and a triple blind study failed to show any effect. In addition, the phenomenon he describes has never been published in a peer reviewed science journal, which almost certainly means that the effect cannot be demonstrated under controlled conditions.

Nevertheless, Dr Emoto showed us how water is energy capable of more than we ever imagined. He hinted that perhaps human thoughts, sounds, and intentions have the power to strengthen or disempower. Through his work we might question that if water is affected by the words, intentions, and energies, what about human beings, which are mainly made of water? Or about other types of particles?

From a Quantum Psychology perspective, there is no question that Dr Emoto's work revealed fundamental properties of the power of our consciousness that are hidden to the naked eye. However, the concerns raised around the methodology are too great to take the original interpretation as it is. Perhaps the results observed were interpreted from the wrong perspective, just as in the parable about the blind men and the elephant.

To expect that water is going to, somehow, be able to understand what a good or bad word is, or which music is supposed to be considered positive and which negative, or to comprehend the cultural attributes of a word written and attached to its container, is just nonsense. However, it was consistently shown that the stimuli (whether positive or negative) generated different outcomes in the frozen crystals. And the results were not different over long distances, as would be expected with entangled particles, as Quantum Psychology claims it.

Perhaps the real fluke in the paradigm was that the power for interpretation and change was assigned to the water itself – that it somehow would be able to interpret the emotional charge of the stimuli and that those would be universal. Instead, we should switch the real power and control over to ourselves. What if it was each researcher, through their individual interpretation of the stimuli, who truly influenced the final outcome of how the water "reacted"?

For instance, Dr Emoto and his team claimed that the water would react negatively to heavy metal music, but what happens if the researcher running that particular sample actually loved that music style? If that person were transmitting good intentions to the water sample while listening to those songs, perhaps the crystals would look just as beautiful as if you applied the pre-assumed positive stimuli. On the same line, it is not the act of writing and attaching a word to the petri that will determine how the water crystals will react, but actually the positive, neutral or negative feeling that those words evoke in the person conducting the experiment.

Perhaps, if you bond or entangle with those samples, you are still able to influence their molecular structure by using the power of your own thoughts and energy. The takeaway from Dr Emoto's experiments would be the possibility that our own (sub) consciousness is able to affect microscopic molecules around us.

Furthermore, Quantum Psychology suggests that if we could control the nature of such energy, we could create better balance in ourselves and the world around us.

7.2. The Psychokinetic Effect Experiment by Helmut Schmidt

Helmut Schmidt (1928-2011) was a German-born physicist and parapsychologist. From the 1960s, Schmidt carried out experiments into clairvoyance and precognition. He pioneered research into the effects of human consciousness on machines, called random number generators or random event generators, at the Rhine Research Center Institute for Parapsychology.

In a typical Psychokinetic (PK) experiment, a random number generator produces a binary aleatory (created by chance) sequence that the subject tries to bias in a certain manner. For example, an experiment is run where in each test run a random generator produces a sequence of 100 light flashes, displayed as either red or green, and the subject in the experiment is instructed to mentally enforce the appearance of more green than red flashes. The sequence of red and green signals is stored, and a score, measured based on the difference between the numbers of red and green signals, is displayed and recorded at the end of each run. When running this experiment Schmidt reported success rates of 1–2% above what would be expected at random over a large number of trials.

The experimental paradigm has been run under different variations, including double blind and delayed result conditions, always showing similar results. Schmidt's work shows the existence of the effect under particularly well-controlled conditions where the participation of independent observers precludes experimenter error, or even fraud. The PK effect appears as an anomalous correlation between the outcome of random events and the mental state of a human subject observing the outcome. The effect is only partly under voluntary control and may depend on subconscious expectations, wishes, and fears of the observer.

Although the effect is usually weak, it may be of practical importance in cases where conclusions have to be drawn from limited statistical evidence. A physicist trying to confirm his own theory experimentally might subconsciously generate a PK effect that could shift the outcome. Similarly, the fear of failure might induce PK effects opposite to the desired direction.

The most challenging aspect of PK is its incompatibility with the classical quantum theory. The experiments indicate that the outcome of quantum jumps, which quantum theory attributes to nothing but chance, can be influenced by a person's mental effort. This implies that current quantum theory is incomplete when experimentally applied to systems that include human subjects. Could Quantum Psychology perhaps fill that gap?

In another set of experiments, Brenda Dunne, the manager of the Princeton Engineering Anomalies Research laboratory, determined to prove what most physicists have never thought possible: that the human mind can change the performance characteristics of machines. Dunne's work showed that consciousness could indeed influence the behaviour of micro-electronic equipment, without the benefit of electrodes or wires. The research shows a tiny but statistically significant result that cannot be attributed to chance.

In her experiments, two-thirds of the participants were able to affect the Random Event Generators (REGs) in the direction they had intended (to select more high or more low numbers), while, according to random probabilities, only half of them would have produced those results by chance. Furthermore, even just sitting an operator in front of the equipment was enough to vary the random outcome, based on the operator's intentions. Dunne also found that the operators didn't even have to be in the same room as the REG to get results; or, for that matter, in the same city, state, or country. Once again, space limitations disappear when we encounter the Quantum Realm combined with our Quantum Self, as it happens when particles are entangled.

Another surprising finding occurred when Dunne and her team asked couples to interact with the REG. The effects generated by two emotionally connected people were much larger than those produced by an "unattached" pair of operators – these results pointed out that interpersonal quantum entanglement have an effect on the physical world around us. Different variations of the original paradigm and equipment have been used over the years, generating the same type of results, and showing that our consciousness has an effect on how reality unfolded during those random exercises.

Sceptics have examined the lab's instruments, its data-processing software and protocols. Environmental, non-consciousness-related influences such as temperature differences, passing traffic, earth tremors, and vibrations from a nearby machine shop have been ruled out as a cause for the anomalies. Dunne has come to believe that human consciousness establishes a "resonance" with the physical world that can reduce some of the randomness around us.

However, Schmidt and Dunne's experiments have a number of detractors. Critics have claimed that Schmidt's experiments have not been replicated. There were weaknesses in the design of the experiments that did not rule out the possibility of trickery. There was little control of the experimenter and unsatisfactory features of the machine employed.

As with Dr Emoto's experiments with water, the criticism has strong grounds. However, there are still important conclusions to be taken from those experiments, which also point towards some of the claims made by Quantum Psychology. Just as with Dr Emoto's conclusions, perhaps the confusion in the interpretation of the results, comes from not focusing in the right details or factors determining them.

Let's go back to when I claimed the missing gap to bring together the macroscopic and the subatomic world might be within Quantum Psychology. From this perspective, the control and power *is* in each one of us, and our unique (sub) consciousness, which allows us to shape the reality of the world unfolding around us. Or, in this case, the results from a random experiment.

Additionally, it is key to mention the importance of strong emotional bonding, which enhanced the results of Dunne's experiment. This effect points out that people in a romantic relationship have a high chance that their energies are entangled, and this fact allows them to generate an even greater impact in their immediate environment. Once more, another odd principle observed in Quantum Mechanics that cannot directly be explained in our macroscopic reality, but could be connected if we view our Quantum Self as the bridge.

Now, let's go one step further. Schmidt and Dunne's experiments made no distinction between the participants, assuming that absolutely everyone could affect the outcomes of the REG in a similar way. However, the strength and influence that we can pull to impact those results could depend on our personal characteristics. Therefore, based in different factors (or *links*), each one of us could have a stronger or weaker effect on the phenomena. What if there is a particular mind-set, or personality trait that determines and correlates with the amount of influence we can exert in the physical world?

7.3. Individual Differences Affecting REG Task Performance by Isaac R. Betanzos

As I mentioned in the chapter on Chain Link Theory, encouraged by the results in Schmidt and Dunne's experiments, for my Master's Degree I tested some of the most basic assumptions made by Quantum Psychology. I already explained the personality traits that I chose as predictors – subjective **W**ell-being, **A**ttributional styles, **C**oping strategies and **O**ptimism, coined together as the WACO personality pattern.

The four WACO personality traits have been widely studied and analysed in different ways, with almost unanimous evidence showing relationships between them. However, studies using the WACO personality traits as predictors of perceived stress, perceived outcome of major negative life events, and of perceived control and influence in REG experiments, were non-existent.

Research had, unsurprisingly, established that the WACO traits are highly correlated: someone generally

133

optimistic towards life is be more likely to use adaptive coping strategies, with an internal attributional style, and generally experience higher levels of well-being. The next step was to test the importance of the WACO personality pattern when facing stressful situations.

The premise was simple: what if our level of perceived stress and control over stressful events is not largely determined by the context we live in, but instead, by a few personality traits? Why, under similar stressful circumstances, do some people feel happy, confident and able to cope, while other individuals experience greater negativity? Results showed a negative relationship between the WACO personality traits and the level of perceived stress when recalling a major negative life event. Similarly, those with a combined higher WACO scores interpreted the outcome of the negative and stressful events as more positive than those with lower values.

However, some limitations need to be addressed. Firstly, the choices participants made when recalling a major stressful and negative life event may not reflect how they would behave if faced with those situations in reality. The person's memory may have been biased, leading to a lower perceived stress level.

Secondly, it was assumed that individuals either have an adaptive personality trait tendency or a maladaptive one. However, for some of the variables tested this assumption may not be appropriate. For instance, both coping styles (approach and avoidant) are not mutually exclusive. Therefore, coping with stress is a dynamic process, and, as some of the negative events participants recalled were out of their control (for example, the loss of a relative), those concerns should be considered.

It was then tested whether someone could exert a stronger or weaker effect in the results of REG experiments, depending on their WACO personality pattern. For the REG task, 100 either red or green randomly generated circles were presented on a screen over 30 seconds. Participants were asked to press the left button of the mouse as fast as possible, claiming that would generate more green circles (which wasn't true since they were generated randomly). To further incentivise them, they were told that if they succeeded and got more green circles than red, they would get a reward.

After the REG task, participants were asked whether they thought they had succeeded in the task or not, and how much in control they felt they had during the activity. The results showed a strong trend indicating that participants with a higher WACO score were more likely to think they had reached the objective of the REG task – even if they couldn't know it for certain, and to have felt in control of the outcome of the task – even if they supposedly weren't.

Furthermore, a correlation showed that those participants with a higher WACO score were actually more likely to have achieved in the REG task, generating more green circles than red by simply consciously wanting it, with a significant probability beyond any reasonable doubt. This suggests that in the results found by Schmidt and Dunne's experiments, individual differences, like the WACO personality pattern, may play a key role; therefore, not all subjects hold the same predisposition to influencing the random event generator.

In light of the results, training to enhance the WACO personality traits can be crucial to increase the impact our Quantum Self has over the world and reality around us. Additionally, adding new variables could help to create a stable and robust model to further explain and predict different health and psychological afflictions before they exist.

Therefore, this evidence points out that our Quantum Self, if balanced with the rest of the *links*, can enable us to have a bigger and more tangible impact on the physical world. From this perspective, Quantum Psychology would act as the bridge between the macroscopic reality unfolded to us, and the quantum world, where different rules for time and space apply. But how big can our individual impact be if combined or entangled with those around us?

7.4. The Global Consciousness Project

The Global Consciousness Project (GCP) is an international effort involving researchers from several institutions and countries, designed to explore whether the construct of interconnected consciousness can be scientifically validated through objective measurement. The project builds on experiments conducted over the past 35 years at a number of laboratories, demonstrating that human consciousness interacts with random event generators, apparently causing them to produce non-random patterns. The principal public face of the Global Consciousness Project is Dr Dean Radin, an electrical engineer and Ph.D. in Psychology.

The GCP's methodology is based on the hypothesis that events, which elicit widespread emotion or draw the simultaneous attention of large numbers of people, may affect the output of random number generators in a statistically significant way. The GCP maintains a network of hardware, which is interfaced to computers at 70 locations around the world. Custom software reads the output of the random number generators and records a trial (sum of 200 bits) once every second. The data are sent to a server in Princeton, creating a database of synchronised parallel sequences of random numbers. The GCP is run as a replication experiment, essentially combining the results of many distinct tests of the hypothesis. The remote devices have been dubbed *Princeton Eggs*.

The researchers aim to show that the behaviour of the network of random sources is correlated with interconnected human consciousness on a global scale. So far there has been a highly significant overall effect on the GCP instrument during special times identified as "global events", which bring great numbers of people to share consciousness and emotions. The effect is a tiny deviation from what's expected, but the patient replication of tests has gradually created very strong statistical support for the reality of this subtle correlation of human consciousness with deviations in random data.

The probability that the effect could be just a chance fluctuation is less than one in a billion. But the correlation is subtle, so much so that individual event results are too weak to be reliably interpreted. However, the GCP effects are not seen primarily as deviations of the individual "eggs", but can be seen as an increase in the average correlation between pairs of eggs separated by distances up to thousands of kilometres. This means that, although the direct effects are too small for us to detect, they occur in synchrony, and this leads to detectable changes in the network as a whole. By definition, the eggs are independent and should not show any relationship at all. However, during moments of importance to humans, the devices show slight correlations with each other.

An array of REG devices in Europe and the United States showed non-random activity during widely shared experiences of deeply engaging events. For example, the funeral ceremonies for Princess Diana, and the 1998 Winter Olympics in Nagano, Japan, created shared emotions and a coherence of consciousness that appeared to be correlated with structure in the otherwise random data. This presents a challenge to status quo physics and Psychology, but is in line with the claims and implications proposed by Quantum Psychology.

There is not a lot of published criticism of Global Consciousness out there to cite, one is that the theory lacks consistent claims that are specific enough to be tested. Despite this criticism, it seems clear that the individual power each one of us holds within our Quantum Self, aggregates and interacts with other people's own consciousness, making the sum greater than its parts. As expected, considering some of the principles from Quantum Mechanics, our entangled energy as a conscious species has an effect on the world that is tangible, yet hard to measure.

But what about the effect our Quantum Self has on other living beings?

7.5. The IKEA "Bully a Plant" Experiment

You have probably heard before that if you talk to your plants, they will grow healthier. The Swedish furniture company IKEA took it a step further in their "Bully a Plant" experiment, designed to raise awareness around bullying. The preliminary question was simple: What happens to a plant if it is bullied? IKEA took two plants and installed them at a school. One plant was then fed compliments and words of encouragement, while the other was verbally bullied with hateful words. Other than the words said, both plants were treated strictly the same: with the same amount water, sunlight and fertilizer.

After 30 days, the results spoke for themselves: while the complemented plant continued to thrive, the bullied plant was visibly struggling, and looking dull with droopy brown leaves.

Although the test was not run in the most scientific environment, it nonetheless showed interesting results. Nevertheless, it was criticized for not being carried out by an impartial research team but by an advertising agency hired to create a powerful social service product to enhance the IKEA image. Despite this, the results hint at the potential of how our Quantum Self, projected into the world, can shape and affect it to a certain degree.

Up until now, I have been insisting on the importance of our consciousness in influencing the physical world through the Quantum Psychology bridge; however, what happens if that power is handed to an extreme external source of energy? One so powerful that it is even capable of annihilating our own natural and Quantum source of energy?

7.6. Radioactivity & Its Effects on Us

Radioactivity is one of the deadliest, yet mysterious, types of energy in our world. Radioactive decay occurs in unstable atomic nuclei – that is, particles that do not have enough binding energy to hold the nucleus together due to an excess of either protons or neutrons. Radioactive decay is determined by quantum mechanics – which is inherently probabilistic. Therefore, it is impossible to work out when any particular atom will decay, but we can make predictions based on the statistical behaviour of large numbers of atoms. Although some radioactive materials are produced artificially, many occur naturally and result in a certain amount of radiation in our environment all the time – this is known as "background radiation".

Some gamma radiation comes from space as cosmic rays. Other radiation comes from sources in the atmosphere, such as radon gas and some of its decay products. There are also natural radioactive materials in the ground, as well as the obvious elements such as uranium. There are also radioactive isotopes of common

142

substances such as potassium and carbon. To understand how much background radiation is around, it helps to distinguish between effects on normal matter and on the human body.

There are two main health effects caused by radiation, which act over the short and long term, and also at shorter and greater distances. Radiation causes health problems by killing cells in the body, and the amount and type of damage depends on the dose of radiation received and the time over which the dose is spread out. At high levels, exposure is likely to cause symptoms of radiation poisoning, such as nausea and damage to organs including bone marrow and the lymph nodes. Larger doses will cause haemorrhaging, sterility and skin to peel off, and extremely high doses are fatal.

Receiving a high dose in a shorter time usually causes more acute damage, as greater doses kill more cells, while the body can have had time to repair some damage with more time having elapsed between doses. However, radioactive material that is spread to a wider area can cause longer-term health effects via prolonged exposure, particularly if they enter the food chain or are inhaled or ingested directly.

Nuclear radiation, unlike the radiation from a light bulb or a microwave, is energetic enough to ionize atoms by knocking off their electrons. This ionizing radiation can damage DNA molecules directly, by breaking the bonds between atoms, or it can ionize water molecules and form free radicals, which are highly reactive and also disrupt the bonds of surrounding molecules, including DNA.

If radiation changes DNA molecules enough, cells can't replicate and they begin to die, which causes the immediate effects of radiation sickness – nausea, swelling, hair loss. Cells that are damaged less severely may survive and replicate, but the structural changes in their DNA can disrupt normal cell processes – like the mechanisms that control how and when cells divide. Cells that can't control their division grow out of control, becoming cancerous. With ingested particles, some may pass through the body before they do much damage, but others linger.

For example, the Chernobyl accident released a plume of radioactive materials into the atmosphere in a fraction of a second. In the following years, the incidence of thyroid cancer increased among those exposed in Ukraine and nearby countries. People were exposed to radioactive material mainly from eating contaminated leafy vegetables and dairy, and the cancer only showed up between four and ten years after the accident.

Without question, radioactive atoms have serious effects on our health. However, some particularities suggest a subtle connection between radioactivity effects and Quantum Psychology: firstly, the individual differences in the extent of effects suggest that certain factors or *links* might influence the level of harm caused, even under extreme radiation; secondly, the fact that radiation, which belongs to the microscopic world, affects us in such a biological and physical way, shows that to some extent we are interacting with the Quantum Realm.

Therefore, we are retro influenced by the subatomic laws where, as you know, time and space doesn't apply the same way as in our macroscopic plane. Does radioactivity hint that our (sub) consciousness can act as the bridge to bring the macro and subatomic realities together? What about other life forms where self-awareness and consciousness are not as developed as in humans? Since our Quantum Self can be perceived as an evolutionary advantage, perhaps other species have learnt ways to adapt to their environment by maximising the benefits of their Quantum Psychology experience.

7.7. The Quantum Self in Wildlife

So far, we have covered evidence pointing towards some of the implications of Quantum Psychology, but always from a human perspective. However, the connection between live beings and the Quantum Realm is not only applicable to humans, as it is the most basic ingredient for life. In fact, every single living being in the Universe has a Quantum Self.

Just as default senses differ between species, so does the way we perceive and interact with ourselves at a Quantum level, or, in fact, with every other being and the physical world. Moreover, some species have developed very complex ways to maximise the biological benefits from connecting with this seemingly odd Quantum reality, helping them to develop and adapt to their environment.

For example, let's consider the synchronisation of a flock of flying starlings, called a murmuration. When starlings fly in this magnificent coordination, it usually indicates the presence of a predator hovering around them. Thus, murmuration is a phenomenon that is mostly triggered out of instinctive defence. Studies suggest that a flock of birds is never led by a single individual, the fluidity of motion is governed by each and every bird, and even the slightest change in the direction and speed of one bird will convey a message to the entire flock to move accordingly.

If the flock were to follow a single leader, or their neighbour, the reaction time required of each bird to follow that trend would have to be very fast – faster than birds actually do react, according to scientists who have studied the reaction times of individual birds in laboratory settings. Instead, they *anticipate* sudden changes in the flock's direction of motion, and this then spreads through the flock in a wave. Traditional science hasn't yet been able to explain how birds are able to synchronise faster than their biological brain allows them to.

From a Quantum Psychology perspective, it could be explained as a highly adaptive form of biological Quantum Entanglement that allows them to protect themselves from predators, and therefore to survive. This way, the flock of birds are able to have an exceptionally developed quantum connection amongst the group, allowing them to instantly communicate and coordinate the direction of their flights.

Similar to a flock of birds, shoals of fish have developed behaviour that could be seen as quantum connection patterns, but in an even more complex way. Research claims that fish in large groups make better decisions than individuals or small groups. It turns out, the amazing synchronised swimming that fish in shoals exhibit is actually caused by each fish using very simple rules to respond to its neighbours. These rules include: 'accelerate towards a neighbour that is far away from you' and 'decelerate when a neighbour is right in front of you'. However, the model admits limitations where some synchronised moves don't fit the model. This is where Quantum Psychology could fill the gap: another ingredient in such a complex form of communication that separates life from death for the members of the shoal.

Truly amazing quantum connections are not only found in more developed organisms, but also in small insects. Take a colony of ants for instance. Generally speaking, ants live in complex social colonies, with the queen being the leader and the workers foraging and protecting their home. Ant colonies can be formed by millions of specimens, covering territories spanning kilometres. Ants not only have amazing defence mechanisms to ensure that all the members of their colony are safe, but they also employ a novel method to increase and further extend their colonies.

In appearance, and despite having such huge colonies, ants do not give orders to other ants. In fact, there is no way in which an ant can direct the actions of another ant. The most striking feature in the management of ant colonies is that there is no management. There is no central power structure outside of the queen; queen ants are leaders of sorts, but they still do not order or explicitly instruct other ants to do anything.

Scientists have been studying the social behaviour of ants and other insects for decades, searching for chemical cues and other signals that the insects could use to coordinate such complex actions. Much of this work has focused on understanding how ants decide where to forage or build their homes. New research, combining observations of ant behaviour with modern imaging techniques and computational modelling, is beginning to reveal the secrets of ant construction. It turns out that ants perform these complex tasks by obeying a few simple rules.

Guy Theraulaz, a behavioural biologist at the Research Centre on Animal Cognition in Toulouse, France, and his team have analysed videos of ants crawling across petri dishes as they attempt to build a shelter, noting each time that an ant picked up or dropped off a grain of sand. The researchers discovered three main rules: the ants picked up grains at a constant rate, approximately two grains per minute; they preferred to drop them near other grains, forming a pillar; and they tended to choose grains previously handled by other ants, probably because of marking by a chemical pheromone.

The researchers used these three rules to build a computer model that mimicked the nest-building behaviour. In the model, virtual ants moved randomly around a three-dimensional space, picking up pieces of virtual sand soaked in a virtual pheromone. The model ants created pillars that looked just like those made by their biological counterparts. The researchers could alter the pillars' layout by changing how quickly the pheromone evaporates, which could explain why different environmental conditions, such as heat and humidity, influence the structure of ant nests.

However, the researchers noted some limitations to their model. For example, there is the case of a model of desert ants that re-created their complex foraging expeditions without the need for a chemical trail marker, created at a time when scientists had found no evidence for one. Also currently missing is an evolutionary approach to understanding the ant behaviour. However, the complex organisation found in insects with a limited developed nervous system, such as ants, could be understood if we added more factors into the equation, such as climate conditions, DNA or, of course, Quantum Psychology.

Adding the quantum factor into the equation, it seems that ant colonies have developed ways to organise and coordinate complex social structures by biologically entangling themselves. Said entanglement would appear not only in situations of basic survival or protection from predators (as birds and fish do), but to overcome complex obstacles.

Finally, there is another insect species with communication and organisation systems in place, which has developed in complex ways in order to survive and thrive: bee colonies and beehives. A honeybee colony typically consists of three kinds of adult bees: workers, drones, and a queen. Several thousand worker bees cooperate in nest building, food collection, and brood rearing. However, surviving and reproducing take the combined efforts of the entire colony. Individual bees cannot survive without the support of the colony. A colony normally has a single queen and several hundred drones during late spring and summer. The social structure of the colony depends on an effective system of communication.

Bees have their own language that is very different from our own. They dance to tell others where nectar and pollen are, how much there is, and if it is high quality. However, this explanation falls short when it comes to understanding how thousands of bees can coordinate themselves in such smooth way.

In fact, honeybee colonies are 'superorganisms'. A superorganism is an organised society or group consisting of many individuals, that together function as a whole unit. This efficient organisation of a colony is vital for the survival and success of the honeybee and is possible as a result of the highly cooperative structure of honeybee societies. In every moment in the life of a colony a tremendous number of stimuli is perceived, thousands of solutions have to be found, decisions are taken and – of course – many thousands of reactions follow. But who decides what has to be accomplished, when and in which way? Surprisingly, it is completely self-organised.

Self-organisation is a property of many complex systems that consist of a great amount of interacting subsystems. One characteristic of self-organisation is a spontaneous forming of structures and patterns under specific conditions. Each individual works (blind to the holistic pattern) to the local rules, the overall pattern results from the interaction of these single individuals. Every single bee has the ability to perceive only a little part of the entirety of influencing stimuli, but the whole of bees appears as a "collective intelligence". A honeybee colony operates as a parallel processing system in which decision-making is performed simultaneously by largely independent working individuals.

Therefore, as a way to be able to interact and thrive as a species, bees have developed a complex multi-channel communication system. Added to all the factors involved in their organisation, we must consider their ability to have a quantum entanglement throughout the beehive. And, unlike ants, their quantum connection seems to be more focused on finding nectar and resources or communicating in smaller groups.

7.8. Wrapping Up

In light of all the information presented in this chapter, there are a few things we should take into consideration. First of all, most of the presented experiments are generally considered as pseudoscience and not as conclusive evidence whatsoever. Heavy criticism has been raised, although a shift towards a Quantum Psychology perspective might palliate some of those limitations.

If you reflect on the claims made by the experiments mentioned here, and the results shown by Quantum Mechanics without the Quantum Psychology lens, we then would have two conflicting realities: on one side, all the laws and odd discoveries made by Quantum Physics, which haven't yet been fully explained by focusing on subatomic particles alone; on the other side, evidence showing that there is some effect in the physical world caused by our own (sub) consciousness, where the laws of Quantum Mechanics (and not the macroscopic laws) seem to be at play.

To further understand the first reality, we need to consider and even further challenge what we know and assume to be true about reality. For all we know, nothing can travel faster than the speed of light, and this seems to be an unchallengeable truth. However, what if information in the subatomic world actually travels faster than the speed of light, bending time and space, and resulting in the odd behaviour seen in subatomic particles?

As for the second reality, we have already linked each result with some of the principles and claims made by Quantum Psychology. This new approach could bring those experimental paradigms from pseudoscience into a more robust, tangible and replicable approach.

Finally, and as a tip to bring both realities together, I stand clear stating that we, as conscious beings, through Quantum Psychology, are the bridges that unite both worlds (macro and subatomic), tackling some of the biggest riddles in Psychology and Physics.

It is that power, which lies within each one of us, that connects us with reality. It allows us to impact how the world unfolds to us from a classical macroscopic perspective, but also in a subatomic plane, bending the concepts of time and space. Therefore, we, as conscious beings, become the central piece in the puzzle to understand why the Universe is the way it is and how it unfolds when forced to leave the probabilistic Quantum Realm and land into immediate and definite reality.

And, at the core of all that unravelled and powerful energy contained within your (sub) conscious, lies the strongest of all feelings giving sense and driving it: love. However, we will talk more about that when we answer some of the biggest questions that there are when we use the lens of Quantum Psychology: what happens when we die? What is the ultimate meaning of life? What is the origin of the Universe and life? Where is God in all this?

Before that, let's explore further evidence of the existence of our Quantum Self.

CHAPTER 8: THE ESOTERIC AND PHILOSOPHICAL TRAIL TOWARDS QUANTUM PSYCHOLOGY

We have already explored how different experiments point towards some of the claims made by Quantum Psychology. Even if they weren't exempt of controversy and criticism, the results are robust enough to indicate that *something* is happening that cannot be fully explained by traditional scientific theories.

However, in order to present a truly holistic perspective, it is also necessary to present other esoteric and philosophical perspectives in order to cover the trails of connection to our Quantum Self. Once more, please do not take the results as immovable. You should use this evidence to build your personal interpretation of the subject.

Moreover, it is only by embracing a holistic approach that Quantum Psychology will advance. As that part of our consciousness is the key to connect the missing dots of how reality unfolds, it needs to be informed by seemingly distant, yet related, topics and theories.

8.1. Neuro-Linguistic Programming (NLP)

Neuro-Linguistic Programming (NLP) uses perceptual, behavioural and communication techniques to make it easier for an individual to change their thoughts and actions. Richard Bandler and John Grinder developed NLP in the 1970s; they believed it was possible to identify the patterns of thoughts and behaviours of successful individuals and to teach them to others.

NLP is founded on the idea that people operate by internal "maps" of the world that they learn through sensory experiences. NLP tries to detect and modify the unconscious biases or limitations of an individual's map of the world. It operates through the conscious use of language to bring about changes in someone's thoughts and behaviour.

For example, a central feature of NLP is the idea that a person is biased towards one sensory system, known as the preferred representational system or PRS. Therapists can detect this preference through language. Phrases such as "I see your point" may signal a visual PRS. Or "I hear your point" may signal an auditory PRS. An NLP practitioner will identify a person's PRS and base their therapeutic framework around it. The framework could involve rapport-building, information-gathering, and goal setting.

Determining the effectiveness of NLP is challenging for several reasons. NLP has not been subject to the same standard of scientific rigor as more established therapies, such as cognitive behavioural therapy. The lack of formal regulation and NLP's commercial value mean that claims of its effectiveness can be anecdotal or supplied by an NLP provider. So, despite more than four decades of its existence, neither the effectiveness of NLP or the validity of the theories has been clearly demonstrated by solid research.

However, an important contribution made by this practice is its central claim that people are not broken. According to NLP we simply respond to inner communication, whether or not we're aware of it.

Therefore, if you're picturing bad things, you're going to feel tense. And, according to this approach, that means you are working perfectly. When you become aware of how you are perfectly creating a mind-set you don't want, you can change it.

It is here, in the switch to handing the power over to ourselves, claiming that what you believe can be extremely powerful, where Quantum Psychology comes into play. For example, it is helpful to make your goals positive; focus on what you want to have, not what you would like to lose or not have. It is much easier to get motivated about a goal that really satisfies you, so it is better to think about what it is that you really want. For instance, you do not actually want to *buy* your dream house; you want to *live* in it. Additionally, our minds actively look for answers to questions. With NLP the key is to ask the right questions remembering the danger and power contained within our desire to always be right.

NLP touches on some of the *links* within the Linked Chain Theory. However, it stays in a very conservative and limited corner of the spectrum. It doesn't cover how those factors correlate and retro-influence other aspects of our life, such as genetic predisposition, health, social situation or, of course, the Quantum Self.

From a Quantum Psychology point of view, the way we interact with the world around us at a subatomic level has a strong influence in the way we will operationalise and form all our external communications. Therefore, having a deeper understanding of the depth to which we connect with the Quantum Realm, will allow NLP to draw more robust and consistent results, and provide a more individualised approach.

At the same time, Quantum Psychology can benefit from some of the claims and techniques of NLP to help us better attune to our social environment and ourselves. By doing so, we increase our control and impact at a quantum level. At the end of the day, if we feel more satisfied with our social relationships, we generate stronger and deeper Interpersonal Quantum Entanglements, increasing our capacity to influence how life is revealed to us.

8.2. Reiki & Energy Healing

Energy healing, in various forms, has been used for centuries. Advocates of these practices claim that it works with the energy fields of the body. Just as saliva with open wounds, it seems that the energy or heat coming out of our hands holds some sort of healing power. In this case, such healing would work with certain inner physical pains where there is no blood, such as back or joint pain.

It's been reported that certain people can ease discomfort by merely applying their hands over an area of pain. However, other factors should be taken into consideration, for example, the suggestion and expectation that the pain would actually be reduced could be affecting the subjective perception. Either way, it seems clear that, for the purpose of healing or relieving pain, we transmit a very unique and strong type of energy through our hands, most likely quantum connected.

However, as for everything else, there are individual differences in the degree or healing ability that each person holds. And also, as usual, there is always room for improvement and training if it's a skill you are particularly interested in developing.

One of the most popular techniques to channel energy healing is Reiki. Reiki is a Japanese technique for stress reduction and relaxation that also promotes healing. It is administered by "laying on hands" and is based on the idea that an unseen "life force energy" flows through us and is what causes us to be alive – or, from a Quantum Psychology perspective, our Quantum Self. If one's "life force energy" is low, then we are more likely to get sick or feel stress, and if it is high, we are more capable of being happy and healthy. The word Reiki is made of two Japanese words – Rei, which means "God's Wisdom or the Higher Power" and Ki, which is "life force energy". So, Reiki is actually "spiritually guided life force energy."

It is said that the aforementioned spiritual guidance enables the Reiki to flow through the affected parts of the subject's energy field and charges them with positive energy. It raises awareness in and around the physical body where negative thoughts and feelings are contained. This causes the negative energy – such as stress, anxiety, physical pain, sadness, confusion, etc. – to loosen its grip, allowing the touch of the Reiki healer to clear the energy pathways.

According to practitioners, the healing effects are mediated by channelling the universal energy known as qi (or ki). This is the same energy involved in tai chi exercise. It is the life force energy that some believe surrounds all of us. This energy is said to permeate the body. Reiki experts point out that, while this energy is not measurable by modern scientific techniques, those who are attuned to it can feel it.

Some controversy surrounds Reiki, as that it is hard to prove its effectiveness through scientific means, and it should consider factors such as the placebo effect in patients. However, it seems like a technique that is able to treat some types of pain, and maximises our natural ability to do so. Nevertheless, Reiki could benefit and be further explained by a Quantum Psychology perspective. Once both approaches are connected and learn from each other, we will be in the position to design more accurate and powerful ways to channel that energy, mastering our full self-healing potential. For instance, through Quantum Interpersonal Entanglement, we will be able to depict the mysteries and riddles coming from how the qi works in Reiki, its nature, properties, flows, and full potential healing power, from a scientific and measurable perspective.

8.3. Chakras

Odds are, if you've attended a yoga class, group meditation, or indulged in an hour-long reiki session, your instructor or practitioner most likely mentioned your chakras. Literally speaking, the word "chakra" from Sanskrit translates to "wheel" or "disk," but the term references a spiritual energy centre within the human body. The chakra system originated in India between 1500 and 500 BC and is described in the Vedas, the most ancient Hindu scripture. Each chakra corresponds to specific organs as well as physical, emotional, psychological, and spiritual states of being that influence all areas of life.

There isn't much Western scientific evidence that translates spiritual energy into physical manifestations; however, the study of the seven chakras is rooted in the belief that when the chakras are open and aligned, our energy is constantly free flowing, allowing the qi to flow through them. This is because the life force, or qi, that moves inside of you is spinning and rotating. This spinning energy has seven centres in the body, starting at the base of your spine and moving all the way up to the top of your head. In a healthy, balanced person, the seven chakras provide exactly the right amount of energy to every part of your body, mind, and spirit. If one of your chakras is too open and spinning too quickly, or if it is too closed and moving slowly, your health will suffer.

The first three chakras, starting at the base of the spine are chakras of matter, which are more physical in nature. The fourth is the connection between matter and spirit, and the last three are known as chakras of spirit.

First Chakra: The *Muladhara* is the chakra of stability, security, and our basic needs. It encompasses the first three vertebrae, the bladder, and the colon. When this chakra is open, we feel safe and fearless. It is associated with the colour red.

Second Chakra: The *Svadhisthana* chakra is the centre of creativity and sexuality. It is located above the pubic bone, below the navel, and is responsible for our creative expression. It is associated with the colour orange.

Third Chakra: The *Manipura* chakra means lustrous gem and it is the area from the navel to the breastbone. The third chakra is our source of personal power. It is associated with the colour yellow.

Fourth Chakra: The *Anahata* chakra is located at the heart centre; it is at the middle of the seven and unites the lower chakras of matter and the upper chakras of spirit. The fourth is also spiritual but serves as a bridge between our body, mind, emotions, and spirit. The heart chakra is our source of love and connection. It is associated with the colour green.

Fifth Chakra: The *Vishuddha* chakra is located in the area of the throat. This is our source of verbal expression and the ability to speak our highest truth. The fifth chakra includes the neck, thyroid, and parathyroid glands, jaw, mouth, and tongue. It is associated with the colour blue.

Sixth Chakra: The *Ajna* chakra is located in between the eyebrows. It is also referred to as the third eye chakra. *Ajna* is our centre of intuition. We all have a sense of intuition, but we may not listen to it or heed its warnings. It is believed that opening the sixth chakra will help you hone this ability. It is associated with the colour purple.

Seventh Chakra: The *Sahaswara* chakra or the thousand petal lotus chakra is located at the crown of the head. This is the chakra of enlightenment and spiritual connection to our higher selves, others, and ultimately, to the divine. It is associated with the colour white.

The mechanisms for how our energy flows within us and into the Universe are elusive but intriguing. It is no surprise that there is scepticism from a scientific point of view to accept the body of ideas from Reiki and the Chakras. However, they are millenarian techniques that have shown interesting results, indicating how our inner balance affects the energetic message we project into the world. Nevertheless, these techniques lack rigorous explanations of the cycle of that energy, or how it connects with the rest of our body and our environment.

Perhaps we shouldn't take the position, functions, and nature of the chakras in such a pre-determined and invariable way. Energy is flowing and dynamic by nature, and therefore it can be generated in different parts of our body simultaneously, with meaning and cause as individual and unique as each living being.

Quantum Psychology offers insight into how our energy flows and connects our body and spirit with other beings and the world around us. After all, if we are more balanced within ourselves and capable to communicate that balance in the energetic message of our Quantum Self, it will enable us to generate strong and adaptive Interpersonal Quantum Entanglements with others.

Connections of the Quantum Self would then resonate with many other *links* at a more biological level, impacting our health, cognitive perception, epigenetics... Nevertheless, can our Quantum Self, or energetic composition, also affect the physical objects around us and vice versa?

8.4. Feng Shui

We do not only have a direct connection with the energy we generate from within, but also with the energy around us, whether it comes from others or our physical environment. Therefore, even the physical disposition of our environment can affect the way our Quantum Self develops and works. This influence, between the subatomic and the macroscopic world, runs both ways and is channelled by our Quantum Self. This is, in a way, what Feng Shui proposes.

Feng shui is an ancient art and science that was formalised in China over 3,000 years ago. In literal translation *feng* means "wind" and *shui* means "water." In Chinese culture, wind and water are associated with good health, thus good Feng Shui came to mean good fortune.

Feng Shui is sometimes thought to be the art of placement – understanding how the placement of yourself, and objects within a space, affect your life in various areas of experience. It is a complex body of knowledge that teaches us how to balance and harmonise with the energies in any given space – be it a home, office, or garden. Although regarded by some as a pseudo-science, Feng Shui has had an impact on the aesthetics of interior design and the architectural layout of living and working spaces, both in its native eastern and, more recently, Western cultures. There are two key principles in Feng Shui:

Yin and yang: the Taoist theory of yin and yang is essential to Feng Shui. At the core of this principle lies a belief that our lives require a balance of the feminine (Yin) and the masculine (Yang) to maintain a good flow of qi and create a content, happy, successful life. Yin and yang are opposites that are dependent upon one another and which must always be in balance. Discord occurs when one principle outweighs the other.

The five elements: also central to Taoism and Feng Shui is the theory of five elements, wood, fire, earth, metal, and water. By tradition, Feng Shui practice holds that all things consist of varying degrees of these five elements. The five elements can interact in any number of ways, some constructive and some destructive.

There is as much enthusiasm about Feng Shui as there is confusion about it. However, ancient Feng Shui masters knew what quantum physics is telling us today –

that everything around us is composed of endless energy fields connecting everything you see, feel and touch (as well as millions of things we do not see with our physical eyes). This means that if you want to stay healthy, happy, enjoy love and success, your space has to support and nourish this energy. It must be well suited for your personal energy, as well as the energy you want to attract and cultivate. Just like being in the company of a happy person makes your own energy happy, the same happens with your living (or working) space.

As you can see, Feng Shui can be understood as a physical extension of Reiki and the Chakras perspectives, as they even share the same principle and wording for the essential energy of all beings, the qi – or the Quantum Self for us. However, all three techniques seem to be unconnected from one another and they also lack a scientific frame to explain their effects. Nevertheless, their view that energy connects us all, re-affirming our central position as conscious beings, aligns and supports most of the fundamental claims made by Quantum Psychology, and backed up by the laws of the Quantum Realm.

8.5. Meditation

Meditation is an ancient mind and body practice that is estimated to date back as far as 5,000 BCE. It is believed that meditation originated in India, with the earliest documented records of the practice deriving from the teachings of Vedantism – an ancient Hindu philosophy.

In general, meditation involves training the mind to induce a state of consciousness that promotes a sense of serenity and increased concentration. There are numerous forms of meditation, though most fall into four groups: concentrative (focusing the mind on a single object), open awareness (induce a sense of awareness without focusing on a specific object), mindfulness (combining both open awareness and concentration) and guided meditation (using imagery, sounds and/or in-person guidance in order to induce a serene state of mind).

Meditation is commonly used to reduce anxiety and stress, but increasingly, researchers have found the benefits of meditation may have a much wider reach. Consciousness is often likened to a stream, shifting and changing smoothly as it passes over the terrain.

Meditation is one deliberate means of changing the course of this stream, and in turn, altering how you perceive and respond to the world around you. While experts do not yet fully understand exactly how meditation works, research has clearly demonstrated that meditative techniques can have a range of positive effects on overall health and psychological well-being.

There are many things in life that are beyond our control. However, it is possible to take responsibility for our own state of mind – and to change it for the better. By engaging with a particular meditation practice, you learn the patterns and habits of your mind, and the practice offers a means to cultivate new, more positive ways of being. With regular work and patience these nourishing, focused states of mind can deepen into profoundly peaceful and energised states of mind. Such experiences can have a transformative effect and can lead to a new understanding of life.

Using modern technology, like functional magnetic resonance imaging (fMRI) scans, scientists have developed a more thorough understanding of what takes place in our brains while we meditate. The overall difference, compared to a non-meditative state, is that our brains stop processing information as actively as they normally would.

Meditation is a widely used and often self-administered therapy with a long scientific tradition. However, the nature of how it works remains a mystery. If one thing is certain about the mechanisms of meditation, it is that it requires a change in our state of consciousness and energy. Therefore, our Quantum Self being the most basic and elemental form of our consciousness and energy, meditation allows us to establish an enhanced path towards connecting with the Quantum Realm.

By fully understanding how this two-way connection works, we will also comprehend and maximise the benefits of meditation for our health and self-growth.

8.6. Hypnosis

People have been pondering and debating hypnosis for more than 200 years, but science has yet to fully explain how it actually happens. Hypnosis is a trance state characterised by extreme suggestibility, relaxation, and heightened imagination. It is most often compared to daydreaming, or the feeling of "losing yourself" in a book or movie. You are fully conscious, but you tune out most of the stimuli around you. You focus intently on the subject at hand, to the near exclusion of any other thought.

In conventional hypnosis, you approach the suggestions of the hypnotist, or your own ideas, as if they were a reality. If the hypnotist suggests that your tongue has swollen up to twice its size, you'll feel a sensation in your mouth and you may have trouble talking. If the hypnotist suggests that you are drinking a chocolate milkshake, you'll taste the milkshake and feel it cooling your mouth and throat. But the entire time, you are aware that it is all imaginary. Essentially, you are "playing pretend" on an intense level, as children do. The experience of hypnosis can vary dramatically from one person to another. Some hypnotised individuals report feeling a sense of detachment or extreme relaxation during the hypnotic state, while others even feel that their actions seem to occur outside of their conscious volition. Other individuals may remain fully aware and able to carry out conversations while under hypnosis.

One of the best-known theories in the field of hypnosis is Hilgard's neo-dissociation theory. According to Hilgard, people in a hypnotic state experience a split consciousness in which there are two different streams of mental activity. While one stream of consciousness responds to the hypnotist's suggestions, another dissociated stream processes information outside of the hypnotised individual's conscious awareness.

Neuroimaging techniques have shown that highly suggestible people exhibit higher activity levels in the prefrontal cortex, anterior cingulate cortex, and parietal networks of the brain during different phases of hypnosis. These are areas of the brain involved in a range of complex functions, including memory and perception, processing emotions, and task learning. However, the specific brain mechanisms involved in hypnosis are still unclear, though scientists are beginning to piece together the neurocognitive profile of this process.

The practice of promoting healing or positive development through hypnosis is known as hypnotherapy. Hypnotherapy aims to re-program patterns of behaviour within the mind, enabling irrational fears, phobias, negative thoughts and suppressed emotions to be overcome. However, hypnosis may not be appropriate in people with severe mental illness.

As our consciousness is highly involved in the process, in order to explain and control the effects, we need to consider the experience of being hypnotised as a whole, without leaving any part of it out of the equation: this includes our Quantum Self. As Quantum Psychology principles imply, the power of the mind can bend and overrule physical and biological laws. When in an altered state of consciousness, we are more prone to "bend" the macroscopic physical laws, especially those concerning our physical skills and limits.

8.7. The Cell Memory Phenomenon in Organ Transplants

The cell memory phenomenon is a term doctors coined for the personality changes that people undergo after organ transplants. While still not considered scientifically validated, the concept is still supported by several scientists and physicians. The behaviours and emotions acquired by the recipient from the original donor would be explained as combinatorial memories stored in the neurons of the organ donated.

According to Cellular Memory Theory, our personality traits and the parts of us that make us who we are can be stored in various areas of our bodies and not only our brains. When recipients of organ donations report having new personality aspects immediately after recovery it could feasibly be the influences of the personality traits of their donors stored within those organs. Heart transplants are said to be the most susceptible to cell memory. It is a simple enough idea, but it is also a divisive one that challenges the way science perceives the human body.

At the School of Nursing at the University of Hawaii in Honolulu, researchers sought to evaluate whether changes experienced by organ transplant recipients were parallel to the history of the donor. Researchers focused on 10 patients who received a heart transplant and found two to five parallels per patient post-surgery that related to their donor's history. The parallels that were observed in the study were changes in food, music, art, sexual, recreational, and career preferences, in addition to name associations and sensory experiences. In the study, a patient received a heart transplant from a man who was killed by gunshot to the face, and the organ recipient then reported to have dreams of seeing hot flashes of light directly on his face.

Modern science teaches us that the DNA in our

cells is not only the blueprint for the complete design of our physical bodies, but also for our emotional, mental and spiritual state. Furthermore, DNA has mechanisms to cloister environmental and life experiences, such as through epigenetics. So, as we change and grow in any aspect of our lives, our cells are constantly updating our 'personal data'. Cells also retain the information of all life experiences that have been absorbed from genetic heritage, nothing ever experienced whether positive or negative escapes being programmed.

From a Quantum Psychology perspective, the evidence brought by the Cellular Memory Theory seems to pinpoint to a direct connection between our biological self and our Quantum Self, where the line separating the two can often be blurry. Perhaps, as long as a part of us contains life, even if it is not within our body anymore, a chunk of our soul or Quantum Self remains as an indivisible part of that organ. In this case, including the quantum factor could allow us to understand the implications and borders of our own existence.

This is an idea we will further explore when we talk about what lies beyond death. As we will soon learn, the Cell Memory Theory might be hinting us towards answering one of the biggest questions that has ever been asked: what is left of us when we die?

You may not be content with the mystical explanations for all the perspectives covered in this chapter. Quite the opposite, we need to tackle them from a plausible scientific perspective that will allow us to fully develop them. The smallest insight may open up our understanding to how reality unfolds. Quantum Psychology may hold the key to unveiling what is really happening in these "mystical" therapies and techniques. If Quantum Psychology is able to explain and connect them, we will unlock a new potential as a species, one that is already within ourselves, but has remained in the dark of our conscious awareness.

CHAPTER 9: WHAT HAPPENS WHEN YOU SLEEP?

Sleeping is a very curious experience. No one can be certain about why we sleep and dream; yet, we couldn't live without it (figuratively and literally). There are different theories and approaches that try to unravel the physiological mechanisms of sleeping and dreaming as well as the meaning that dreams might hold to our consciousness. However, none of them have been compelling enough to open all the doors towards a universal explanation. Nonetheless, dreams are an interesting insight into our minds, with each dream, in a particular moment, holding a very different meaning for each person, even with dreams that might appear to be identical.

The unique individuality when interpreting dreams makes it extremely difficult to draw general conclusions that can be applied to the broad majority of humankind. Just as our experiences, perceptions, and judgements are individual and unique, the meaning that a dream can have in our own psyche can be very different from one person to another. Furthermore, even within the same person, but at a different time, the same dream can represent very different things.

Nevertheless, why do we dream about something in particular? Why do we sometimes remember them and other times we don't? What's the purpose of dreaming? How can dreams sometimes foresee things yet to occur? Those are questions that have captured our imagination for centuries, often tied up with mysticism and almost magical explanations.

Perhaps Quantum Psychology could cast some light on these riddles. It is generally accepted, and almost intuitive, to feel that some dreams give us a very unique and direct connection to a hidden part of our consciousness and reality. Perhaps when we sleep we are able to connect with a higher part of our Quantum Self, once all the *"biological and social noises"* are switched off.

Before going deeper into the nature and power of dreaming, let's review what happens to us when we fall asleep. Even if you feel like you just conk out until morning, a night of sleep has a typical structure. Most people are familiar with Rapid Eye Movement, or REM, sleep. Before that dream-heavy period, though, we undergo Non-Rapid Eye Movement, or NREM, sleep, which takes up 75% of sleep time and is divided into four stages.

Stage 1 finds us dozing off, with our brain waves and muscle activity slowing down. Some people would call that sleep but, when woken during Stage 1 and asked if they were asleep, about 80% of people will say they were not. Usually comprising about half of sleep time, Stage 2 means a calmer brain wave pattern and no eye movements, slow breathing and slightly lower body temperature. A person in Stage 2 has lost touch with his surroundings but can easily be shaken awake.

By Stages 3 and 4, though, waking someone up probably requires an annoying alarm. Breathing slows even more into a rhythm. Blood pressure and body temperature drop again and muscles relax. These two similar stages are called "slow wave sleep", with the slowest of all brain waves. This is the restorative, deep sleep we crave when we are tired. Scientists believe that much of the body's regenerative work, like protein building and hormone release, happens at this stage. Slow wave sleep is what every mother loves to see in her child: just a peaceful, resting body.

About 90 minutes after falling asleep, REM sets in and hypes up the slow wave sleep into a state that's very close to being awake, with brain waves of the same speed or even faster. Most but not all dreams occur in this phase. The heart beats quickly, blood pressure rises, eyes dart around and breathing becomes rapid and shallow. The body is more or less paralysed; arm, leg, and facial muscles might twitch, but the body will not move. REM can last from five to 30 minutes.

Hormones, chemicals and regions of the brain interact to drive the sleep cycle. The body's biological clock, or circadian rhythm, synchronises a person's sleep schedule with the day/night cycle.

Adenosine is a chemical thought to induce sleep. Levels increase during the day, making us sleepier the longer that we are awake in an attempt to reach homeostasis, or the body's preferred "steady state". Once we fall asleep, adenosine levels drop, reducing the need for sleep and eventually prompting us to wake up. Cortisol, known as a stress hormone, follows a reverse path.

One of the vital roles of sleep is to help us solidify and consolidate memories. As we go about our day, our brains take in an incredible amount of information. Rather than being directly logged and recorded, however, these facts and experiences first need to be processed and stored; and many of these steps happen while we sleep. Researchers have also shown that after people sleep, they tend to retain information and perform better on memory tasks.

Coming back to the questions previously raised, the reason we dream about one topic and not others may depend on different variables: what we are more actively and consciously thinking about, an on-going situation in our subconscious, a conclusion our Quantum Self already reached but which hasn't made its way into our conscious awareness yet, or merely pure coincidence. The rule of thumb I apply when thinking about dreams is: every dream might hold an important meaning, yet not all apparently meaningful dreams will have a true corresponding important meaning behind them.

How is this possible? Well, it's simple: what we dream depends in great measure on what parts of our brain are activated during the dreaming phase of our sleep. Sometimes the part of the brain activated will be more related to memories, other times to desires and wishes, other times to fears, and sometimes to the part of our subconscious that works out problems and issues, which helps us to understand and solve them from a different angle.

However, once a specific part of the brain is activated during the recovery process of sleeping (which is a bit more aleatory), it will increase the chances of the dream going one way or another, meaning: if you are really hungry and you only spend your day thinking about food, chances are you will also dream about a nice meal because the neuron connections in your brain, which represent food, are strong, extended and fresh. Therefore, in this particular situation, there will be more chances that the active part of the brain when dreaming will be focused on food more than on unicorns, for example. This explains why, when you are thinking a lot about a problem that worries you, you will most likely also dream about that topic. In this case you may even be deceived by a confirmation bias by confusing the meaning of your dream with a huge revelation provided by your Quantum Self, even if it's not.

So, how do we recognise when a dream is the result of randomness, or an on-going situation, or an epiphany from your subconscious? Well, to be honest, it is quite hard to know. For now, all we can do is listen to the soul, the gut instinct, raw wordless feelings that crawl from within before we even have a chance to define them as positive or negative. Even though this technique also gets blurry sometimes, especially when feelings are involved.

To make it even more complicated, you also need to take into consideration that dreams are also influenced by that big misleading psychological force: the desire to always be right. For example, if you really want to be right about that person with whom you don't really get along, chances are that you will dream about that person doing something horrible, which will reinforce your dislike towards him or her.

This is why we always need to keep a cool mind and a safe distance when it comes to dreams. Because, although they do hold a great power to hint at hidden parts of ourselves and, in a way, into things that could happen, they are also filled with subjectivity, dissonances and biases.

To understand why can we remember some dreams and not others, or forget them soon after we wake up, the answer is pretty straightforward: it's just a matter of luck (or bad luck, depending on the dream). The phase of sleep, the neuron connections established at the moment the dream takes place, and the importance our consciousness gives to the dream itself, will impact our chances of remembering it. Furthermore, genetics, hormones or environmental factors can also play a role.

Additionally, it is hard to firmly state what the purpose of dreaming is. From a health point of view, it is clear that sleeping helps to reset the brain and if it doesn't take place, the consequences are severe (hallucinations can begin after only 72 hours without sleep); sleeping seems a chemical or physiological consequence of that reset. But we still don't know why we dream, some researchers propose that as we aren't required to focus on anything during sleep, our brains make very loose connections and the images and emotions from the day battle out in our dreams.

Others believe that dreams don't really serve any function at all, that they are just a by-product of the brain firing while we sleep. Either way, dreams can be a good indicator of what is troubling our minds the most. By understanding what thoughts are occupying our minds while we sleep we can choose where to prioritise focus, energy, or work on ourselves based on the feedback from our own mind during an oneiric episode.

It cannot be denied that certain dreams anticipate things that have not yet happened. Almost everyone has had those types of dreams where something happens that is then replicated in the real world. However, we need to distinguish between different types of "foreseeing dreams": it could only be a deja vu, which is likely provoked by a chemical reaction or neuronal connection pattern in the brain that is similar to a previous experience, making you experience a mix between both.

It could also be part of your awareness showing you the solution to a puzzle where you already have all the pieces, yet you have not consciously put them together. Because, when you dream, there are no environmental distractions: you only have light on that part of the brain where the dream is taking place.

Finally, and the most interesting type of foreseen dream to me, are those that directly connect with your Quantum Self. And, since Quantum Physics is ruled by laws where time and space are not linear, in this realm you can jump across time, foresee things that are likely to happen within the spectrum of possibilities, or have a brief revelation that connects you with someone close to

189

you. Nevertheless, remember that the subatomic world works in terms of probabilities, not of certainties.

I'll give you a couple of examples: have you ever thought or dreamt about someone you haven't seen in years, then you bump into that person shortly after? Perhaps our Quantum Self, following the subatomic laws, has jumped in time to bring you that "memory" that is already very likely to happen. Then maybe, and just maybe, drawing that connection with the most basic matter that makes all of us energetic beings, can hold an unbelievable power to understand ourselves, our life or make crucial decisions based on those intuitions where time or space do not apply.

Sometimes you might have just a brief revelation that can change your perception about yourself, your world, or a situation you are deeply involved with. As we discover and gain awareness about the way we connect with others in meaningful ways, bending the rigid rules of time and space to do so, dreaming might be the widest window we experience during life to understand the depths of our own basic nature.

CHAPTER 10: LIFE, DEATH, REINCARNATION AND BEYOND

Welcome to the boldest, most audacious chapter of the book. Throughout the following pages, we will tackle some of the biggest questions ever formulated, giving a plausible explanation for them from a Quantum Psychology perspective. We will follow a trail that, step by step, will lead us deeper than ever into our own nature, and origin as energetic beings of the universe. It is going to be abstract and daring, challenging everything your evolved survival instinct would have you believe. This is the moment we turn everything we take for granted about where we come from, or why the spectrum of reality exists the way it appears to, upside down. And no path that leads to a worthy conclusion is easy and comfortable.

For some part of it, answers will be simpler and

emptier than might be expected of a 'romantic' or philosophical point of view; at other stages, the ideas will require your full capacity of cognitive abstraction and plasticity, in order to comprehend concepts that are subtle to our conscious awareness.

So get ready, fasten your seatbelt and open your mind, because you are about to step into reality from a perspective never embraced before and jump straight into the *rabbit hole* of existence.

10.1. Death & the Process of Grieving

Grief from the death of a loved one is part of life. Research shows that it can take from one to two years and, with certain deaths, five years, to recover from the grief of a death. With important relationships, one never fully recovers. This is part of being human. Grieving is often only associated with the death of someone close; however, we can also experience grief under other traumatic situations such as events where we experience sentimental loss or detachment, like a break-up, or being let down by a very close friend. Pretty much any major change in our reality comes accompanied by a period of grieving what has passed and adjusting to the new order.

The process of grieving is as individual and unique as we are ourselves, and each person deals with the feeling of loss in extremely different manners. To draw a line depicting the "right" path to follow to heal the soul seems pointless. Allowing yourself to feel your loss, digest it, come to terms about your new reality... seems inevitable. There may be nothing in this world that can prepare you to accept a significant loss. However, in times of grief we often feel deprived of all sense of control, but we can regain some of it by embracing whatever we still have control over.

Mourning is the biological process of the brain and body for healing and recovery from loss. Simply put, grief is an extremely emotional experience. Human attachment, as the story of our relationships, is deeply mapped in the limbic cortex. Mourning a death is the change from the deeply held story of a relationship to a new "play", where the loved one is gone. Antidepressants tend to inhibit mourning, numbing out feeling and hardening the personality. But grief is not a brain problem, it is part of the human condition, and pharmaceuticals will never provide a long-term solution.

When you begin the process of mourning, most of your mental attention is directed towards it. Your mind is consumed with disbelief and the struggle to accept your new reality. Your cognitive responses slow down and become muddled, and you may not feel in your "right mind". Research shows that in the early stages of grief mental tasks are deeply affected in many people. You experience a deep biological response to your loss, just as you experience physical, psychological, and emotional responses. Hormones and chemicals are released, internal reactions are disrupted, and important bodily systems shift into emergency mode. Just as the Linked Chain Theory proposes, the shaking of one *link* expands to the rest of the network in tangible ways and to varying degrees.

Grief can be experienced and coped with in many ways. Research by scientist George Bonanno examined people who had experienced the 9/11 terror attacks from up close, for example having lost a loved one. He interviewed and examined them for a period of two years and came to the result that there are four different types when getting over a traumatic experience: the chronic type (permanent psychological or emotional damage resulting from a tragic event), the healed type (people recovered from their initial symptoms that were caused by the traumatic experience), the delayed type (people who didn't experience any significant symptoms until months after the event) and the resilient type (this group only suffered from minor symptoms or even no symptoms at all, after witnessing the horrific 9/11 terror attacks).

But what is the deciding factor that determines whether a person experiences painful symptoms or gets over trauma and pain quickly? It seems that the amygdala, responsible for our assessment of our surroundings looking for potential dangers to put the body in alarm mode, is one of the factors involved. The amygdala can also be oversensitive and detect danger in harmless surroundings and ring the alarm even if there is no danger around. People with a highly sensitive amygdala are therefore at higher risk to suffer from severe symptoms after a traumatic event.

It is common in people to assert that they can feel the presence of a lost person after they passed away. This idea can be embraced from different perspectives: from a religious perspective, where the soul might stay behind to comfort the loved ones; from a psychological point of view, where feeling the presence of the lost person might help to cope with the new situation; even from the philosophical side, depending whether you believe the soul and the body are divided.

In order to further understand the nature and mechanisms of the grieving process, let's follow the quantum trail expanding on how we connect with those close to us. We have already explored the concepts of Quantum Entanglement and how it can be extrapolated to interpersonal and meaningful relationships established during our lifetime – Quantum Interpersonal Entanglement. When you are strongly and deeply entangled with someone else, part of his or her energy becomes part of yours, and vice versa – just as atoms share their properties and fate when entangled. Therefore, although the process of grieving is mostly a cognitive one (accepting the new situation), it is also an energetic or quantum matter.

When someone very close to you dies, you are still entangled to that person, and part of their energy stays with you, often forever. When people claim to feel the presence of someone they have lost, they may be creating a bearable way to accept their loss; or perhaps they are sensitive to the quantum energy of that lost person that still exist in this reality. And, just as neurons can establish connections in our brains that either last for life or fade overtime, so too do our entanglement connections with people close to us persevere.

Let's say for now that death is not the end, that our Quantum Self, a unique energetic imprint of each one of us, is not confined to the limits of our body; similarly, our energy and Quantum Self is not made solely from our energy. As we interact with the Universe and other energetic beings, so does that part of us (call it energy, Quantum Self, spirit, soul...). This type of energy (the basic energy required to be alive) comes from a primary source, which is as old as the universe itself.

Furthermore, when it comes to grieving, we don't always experience it the same way, with intra-differences that rarely follow any logic. For example, you might experience a severe process of grieving for someone you didn't know for that long – or even a pet – and a lesser mourning period for a family member.

Our relationship with death is both universal and individual, and raises questions that have been asked since the dawn of existence: what purpose does death serve and what happens to us when life ends?

10.2. Near Death Experiences

Before we explain the trail we find ourselves on when we die, let's have a closer look at the glimpses we can experience of that trail without fully losing life as we know it. Let's explore those situations where our consciousness is compromised and on the edge between life and death.

Being in a coma

Traditionally put, a coma is a state in which a person is totally unaware of both him/herself and the external surroundings, and unable to respond meaningfully to external stimuli. The word "coma" itself emerged from the Greek for "deep sleep" (koma) around the 17th century. We know now that coma medicine is a deeply complex and neurologically labyrinthine field. So what actually happens, on a basic level, to the body when it is in a coma?

The unconsciousness of a coma comes in a variety forms. A state of prolonged unconsciousness regarded as a coma may be classed as a vegetative state (in which the body makes movements and may grunt or yawn, but has no reaction to stimuli), catatonia (where there's no movement or response of any kind), or brain death (in which the brain function is destroyed, but some of the body's autonomic functions can continue).

Given the different types of coma, there's not a one-size-fits-all example of the brain patterns of comatose people. Consciousness, in the comatose person's brain, appears to have been "turned off" by an interference with the brain's communication between the brainstem and the cerebrum, which controls cognitive consciousness. In the brain of an awake person, thinking for oneself and seeing light or another sensory stimulus would produce neural patterns of activation that are absent in those who are comatose. There is quite a lot we still don't know about the comatose brain.

Now imagine this, you are lying in a hospital bed, in a coma, apparently dead to what is happening around you. But you experience it all the same, hear what is being said about and to you, and try in vain to communicate with your loved ones and the world outside. This is what happened to Ron Houben, a Belgian student who spent 23 years in a so-called persistent vegetative state after being paralyzed in a car crash. Only after two decades did doctors recognise that, though they had concluded that his consciousness was "extinct", his brain was still functioning almost entirely normally.

So, do people actually remember being in a coma? We have already mentioned that there are different types of coma; therefore, it makes sense to expect that the experiences of a coma will also differ. People who have been in comas have reported vivid dreams and hallucinations, in some cases, what's going on around the comatose person is incorporated in these dreams. But what happens with those patients that recall their surroundings and conversations that took place, sometimes even outside the room they were lying in? Those accurate revelations challenge everything we know about consciousness and the limits of life itself.

According to those patients, they experience a certain state of awareness, often like floating, where they don't have memories or the sense of stress or anxiety that we would expect from such an odd situation. Quite the opposite, they feel calm and peaceful, like passive observers, only able to gather the "sensations" of the situation or feel the feelings of those close to them that are present in the room.

From a Quantum Psychology perspective, this helps us to understand the depths of the Quantum

Interpersonal Entanglement we experience with those we love. Additionally, this type of experience might give us a hint of what to expect once we depart the land of the living, but we will dig into that idea a bit later.

Astral Projection

To put it simply, astral projection is often understood as when your soul leaves your body and travels beyond the biological limitations. Some claim that when you are travelling this way, your soul can go anywhere and meet anyone. From this esoteric perspective, when your soul leaves your body, it is attached to a 'cord'. This 'cord' is your lifeline back into your body. When you die, this 'cord' becomes detached, allowing your soul to be free of your physical body.

As a concept in many Eastern cultures, astral projection is found in yoga, Hinduism and Buddhism, among others. Astral projection can happen spontaneously – like in near-death experiences – or it can be experienced through conscious effort. Trauma, illness, or water and food deprivation, as with Native American vision quests, can trigger astral projections. Lucid dream are opportunities for intentional astral projections. With practice and lucidity, awareness can be directed to locations or activities. Neuroscientists are puzzled, while medical professionals no longer dismiss the experience out of hand, science holds the view that astral projections involve neurological or brain dysfunction.

Symptoms and sensations often accompany an astral projection, particularly at the point of separation or disconnection. Some people have reported various phenomena, including but not limited to vibrations, sounds of voices nearby, sleep-paralysis and a 'buzzing' sound in the head. All of these, a combination of them, or even none of these phenomena may occur. Everyone is unique.

The nature or veracity of astral projections remains unclear and its study seems tricky and deceiving. However, from a Quantum Psychology perspective these states can be seen as experiences where we are closer to the part of our (sub) consciousness ruled by the laws of Quantum Mechanics, without needing to die to do so. It is possible that, through thorough training, we are able to master our own consciousness and the weight of its interaction with the quantum world, allowing us to have more control over our own Quantum Self and to benefit from it. From this perspective, astral projections would represent a high-form of connecting with that higher part of our existence and reality.

Anaesthesia

Anaesthesia is a mysterious concept to most of us, even if we have been anesthetised before. The term comes from the Greek for "loss of sensation", but that's not the only effect it causes in the body. Prior to the invention of anaesthesia in the mid-1800s, surgeons had to hack off limbs, sew up wounds and remove mysterious growths with nothing to dull the patient's pain but opium or booze.

Since then, doctors are much better at putting us out with drug combinations that ease pain, relax muscles and, in some cases, put us in a deep state of hypnosis that gives us temporary amnesia. Today there are two primary types of anaesthesia drugs: those that knock out the whole body (general) and those that only numb things locally. We will focus on the former.

General anaesthesia renders patients unconscious with no perception or memory of the surgery. It also limits the physiological responses to surgical cuts. Despite their necessity in modern medicine, scientists aren't exactly sure how anaesthetics work. The most accepted theory suggests that they dissolve some of the fat present in brain cells, changing the cells' activity.

Sometimes, patients under general anaesthesia might experience what is known unintended intraoperative awareness. This refers to rare cases where patients report a state of awareness during an operation, after the point at which the anaesthetic should have removed all sensation. Some patients are conscious of the procedure itself and some can even feel pain.

Researchers have gained new information on brain activity during general anaesthesia by recording changes in the electrical activity of the brain. They discovered that changes in electroencephalogram readings correlated with the loss of consciousness itself and also by the non-specific effects of the drugs.

According to a group of doctors in Finland, it may be that we never fully lose consciousness under anaesthesia. Two new studies suggest that the brain is still partly conscious under the influence of anaesthetics, even though the person who has taken the drug isn't reacting or seemingly aware.

Perhaps, just as it seems to happen when in a coma or during an astral projection, this artificially altered state of our consciousness might hold a way to bring us closer to awareness of our Quantum Self. What is certain is that by depicting near-death experiences we might also get closer to unveiling what happens to us once we leave behind everything we understand as living. But what is the process? What are we able to experience when we perish? Is there a heaven or hell waiting for us, or just the eternal darkness of non-existence?

Let's try to answer the biggest question of them all, by embracing the implications of our Quantum Self to its peak level.

10.3. What Happens After We Die

After providing enough context and framing of the concepts and implications around Quantum Psychology, it is time to present how our Quantum Self can unveil our true position as beings of this reality. As we begin climbing that mountain, we will start by answering one of the most mysterious, devious and transcendent questions ever formulated: what happen to us when we die?

This is a riddle that has mesmerised and terrorised humankind for as long as our history goes back. There are countless interpretations regarding what is waiting for us once all the lights of this world turn off. However, none have gathered enough support or presented a valid scientific path to follow. Some assume that answering it will never be possible; others believe that, if we ever did, our species would be doomed, as there are things that we are not supposed to know.

Although I sympathise with both perspectives and respect any others out there coming from a similar pessimistic view, I just don't agree with them. Every question we are able to formulate can be answered and explained. It's just a matter of finding the right theoretical approach and developing the appropriate techniques for it. Think about it: 500 years ago, when we thought the Earth was flat, the idea of going to the Moon generated a similar fear and disbelief. It was simply unconceivable. However, as society and technology evolved, the impossible crosses to the realm of reality, sparked in the minds of those that can't be discouraged by defeating and conformists echoes.

Quantum Psychology is a story about time, space and profound interpersonal connections, and how those three concepts, which we take for granted, can be deceiving to us, even if their true nature lies right in front of us. And with death, more than with anything else covered in this book, those concepts become even blurrier and more flexible than ever. However, comprehending the cycle of existence is going to be a true exercise of imagination and introspection; one that is likely to challenge the way you understand the world and yourself.

Religious or spiritual points of view have a unanimous belief in the soul or an afterlife plane of reality. The spirit is frequently viewed as capable of leaving the body after we perish and being reborn, for example, as a bird, a butterfly, or an insect. The Venda of southern Africa believe that, when a person dies, the soul stays near the grave for a short time and then seeks a new resting place or another body – human, mammalian, or reptilian.

The concept of spirituality and the afterlife, from which all religions are raised, are as old as human self-awareness itself. Even remote villages, with limited contact with civilization, have a natural way of developing beliefs and rituals about the afterlife, venerating their deaths. Whether it is a cultural factor or a genetic one (where natural selection predisposed us to a notion that perishing is not the end), there seems to be an inherited inclination to expect something more after death. Like we have an instinct that the very same core energy that differentiates us from inanimate objects transcends into eternity. This element is what we call the soul, spirit, energy… or your Quantum Self.

This energy enables life and comes from a single source, filling every single organism and life form in the universe. Our soul or Quantum Self is both individually independent and part of a bigger energy flow that connects all of us, allowing us to connect in meaningful ways through Quantum Interpersonal Entanglements. We cannot separate ourselves from this eternal flow of quantum energy; it is where we all come from and where we will all go.

For instance, Jung proposed what is known as the collective unconscious, sometimes called the objective psyche. It refers to the idea that a segment of the deepest unconscious mind is genetically inherited and is not shaped by personal experience. Jung's theory on the collective unconscious was that it is made up of a collection of knowledge and imagery that every person is born with and is shared by all human beings due to ancestral experience. According to Jung's teachings, the collective unconscious is common to all human beings and is responsible for a number of deep-seated beliefs and instincts, such as spirituality, sexual behaviour, and life and death instincts. Humans may not consciously know of these archetypes, but they hold strong feelings about them.

Whether Jung's theory is the case or not, in order to understand what to expect after death, we need to cover two premises. Firstly, that the representations of the world, fabricated in our minds, and the energetic connections made in this reality, must, to some extent, transcend when we die. Secondly, that in order to unveil the trail towards eternity, another simpler question should be answered first: *what does being alive imply?* By answering it, we can depict and eliminate everything that we lose when our body gives up and we go beyond. If there were nothing left after, then the pessimists would win, and it would mean that our spirit and consciousness disappears, resulting in an eternal night. On the contrary, if we find anything within ourselves as beings that are not dependent of the physical body, then we could understand and glimpse what "being dead might feel like".

It is obvious that when we die, we lose our corporeality. Since we no longer have a body, with its organs and their needs, you no longer need to satisfy all its functions: hunger, thirst, or the rest of the urges and motivations required to maintain a functioning body. Memories would disappear as they are formed and kept by the neuron synapses in your brain, but where you are going you won't need them anyway.

I know that the idea of giving up your memories and identity can be daunting and stressful. However, it makes all the sense in the world. After all, some people even lose memories while alive, for example in Alzheimer patients. Nonetheless they maintain the same core sensations, basic attributes, and energy that enable life, even if these patients cannot attribute them to a particular memory.

Finally, and at a more abstract level, when you die you lose the linear nature of time and space that dominates your existence when you are alive. Just as we saw before, some people have experienced it when going through a coma or during an astral projection, where there is no attachment to the linearity of space and time, and experience is merely a happening, one second at the time. Instead of that, "what's left of us", transcends to a quantum plane where, as we well know, those concepts do not answer to the same rules as the macroscopic world. In this realm you can forget about being a bored or becoming a ghost stressed out about not being able to communicate with anyone.

So, what is left of us then? We have no physical needs, no memories to motivate our actions as a spirit, and we will not even be at a certain place at a given moment either! You are just reduced to the basic essence of your consciousness: your Quantum Self. What is left of us, in this quantum version, are the remains shaped through the connections and the raw sensations that we experience when we are alive, changing that basic form of our energy.

To further comprehend what these raw sensations are, think of that warm energy that awakens inside the very core of your essence when you reunite with someone you love and care after some time apart. Or that feeling of safety and tenderness when you revisit somewhere from your childhood and you are transported to some of the happiest moments of your life. Think of the anger and pain evoked when remembering something or someone who hurt you deeply. Raw sensations are all those moments of bonding, filled with the true emotions that arise within us before they can even are labelled by our conscious mind, memories and expectations. It is this conglomerate of primary gut feelings or reactions that contains the energy of our spirit and connects us to the defining moments, places or beings in life. This is what prevails after our death.

It is when we move into the plane of the afterlife that, just as with certain comatose patients, we no longer have that heavy awareness attached to our bodies and memories, but only a faded and pure version of our energetic selves. Therefore, when we die, we are not fully conscious beings that will be stressed by not being able to interact with our loved ones or crave a favourite meal. All those concepts of existence belong to the macroscopic world and are tied to our biological limitations. The plane of existence that we move into is one where all that remains is our Quantum Self, where we are the compound of our core and raw energy. Moreover, the essence of feelings and Quantum Interpersonal Entanglements made through life are ruled by the principles of Quantum Mechanics – governing and jumping across time and space.

But, once we move into this new plane of existence, what determines where we "jump" or "land" in terms of time and space? Most likely, a wide range of factors, mainly influenced by the true connections and feelings we experience in life – whether our life was ruled by healthy and meaningful relationships, or by toxic and negative ones.

Maybe even at several places and times simultaneously, just as if you could step into different rooms with each of your feet. Based on this, the quality of the relations built and maintained during life are of great importance. What lives on from this lifetime will be shaped by your way of experiencing and embracing certain patterns of emotions and what remains of you when you pass will be impacted by the quality and depth of such connections.

This also implies that there would be as many ways of experiencing the afterlife as there are personalities, since none of us experience our emotional world and connect with our environment in the same way. From this point of view, it is essential to consciously train our mental muscle towards optimism, as this will play a key role in the way our spirits will pass to the next step of existence.

However, we do not move from the living and macroscopic world into this quantum plane instantly. In fact, research shows that the human body can take hours to cool down after dying, and that many different body functions take time to fully shut down. This would also explain the cell memory phenomenon in transplants: since those organs must be removed and preserved straight away, it is likely that part of the core Quantum Self of the deceased person (call it soul or spirit if you must) is still contained within that organ and connected with the unique physiological and genetic make-up of the donor.

The process of moving on to the quantum plane is unlikely to be straightforward for everyone. In fact, how we die would have an impact on the way we step into the next plane, or 'how much' of our Quantum Self moves simultaneously, and as a united chunk of energy, to the afterlife. If death comes in natural and peaceful ways, that transition will be less dramatic, and therefore a "bigger chunk" of your essence will stay together in this quantum plane of existence. On the contrary, if death is sudden and traumatic, some part of our core energy will fade away and be diffused with the rest of the Quantum Energy around us.

Understanding death as a parallel plane of subtle and basic consciousness, where time and space are relative and non-linear, would explain why we sense the presence of those we lose from time to time, often in places that held meaning to that person. However, this sensation will not necessarily mean that the Quantum Self of the person deceased is present, because there is also a psychological bias to take into consideration: there will be occasions where, due to the grieving process, the mind will be "tricked" into feeling the presence of that person, as a coping response to the situation, even if the quantum essence of the person is not present.

Making this even more complex, there is another factor to consider: when we die, we progressively lose that individuality that we hold so dear while we are alive, encouraged by the confines and clear limits of our physical body. When we pass to this quantum plane, even if we maintain most of our essence as a sort of "energetic unit", such essence or spirit is eventually partially or totally dispersed into the torrent of omnipresent energy that connects every single being and object in the universe. Therefore, we lose partly, mostly, or totally, our energetic individuality once we die, but even though we are not fully aware and conscious of our existence, as we are when we are alive, it is something that in any case supposes a source of stress.

The negativity or anxiety that we carry with us when we pass is the very same as that which torments us while we are alive – based on our dysfunctional or unresolved connections. After that, we will respond and cause responses, at a raw emotional level, when in presence of certain stimuli, situations, places, or (especially) people that we connected with during life. This interaction will generate a similar reaction in the core emotions of all parts involved, as it would do when alive.

For example, if your Quantum Self or spirit "lands" in a space and time where the love of your life is, that chunk left of your essence will (hopefully) feel that positivity, love, and happiness that her/his presence evoked to you in life, even though you are interacting on different planes of reality. And, simultaneously, if the person alive is sensitive enough to feel such energies at a quantum level, he/she will have that raw feeling in the gut when briefly reconnecting with that known and beloved energy. Then, brain, memories, and expectations will kick off in the mind of the living person, framing and shaping that raw feeling, often transforming it into a sensation of grief and sadness, even if the primary and automatic reaction was a positive one.

The nature and intensity of such reactions will depend on two main factors: our ability to develop

Quantum Interpersonal Entanglements at an energetic level, and our ability to sense these entanglements.

In terms of developing these relations, the phrase *"you are alive for as long as you are remembered"* embraces a completely new meaning. Because, in fact, we start "losing" that restrained energetic individuality long before we die. From this perspective, every time we connect or entangle with someone in a meaningful way (whether formed by well-adjusted patterns or toxic ones), we will "give up" a portion of our individual energy, which will then be hosted by the other being, and we receive a "chunk" of energy from that other person in return.

However, the entanglement might be unidirectional or non-existing, and there might be times where a relationship will hold a much deeper meaning for one of the parties involved than the other. Once more, inter and intra-individual differences apply. In fact, some of the times we sense someone we lost, it could be that we are sensing the part of that person's energy that still resides within ourselves.

In terms of the specific traits and ability of a person to sense such connections, just like any of our other senses, there are individual differences regarding the accuracy and development of our awareness and use of the Quantum Self and its connections. Just like any other skill, it can be consciously trained; therefore, our own essence and energy don't belong only to us, but make up the fabric of society as we grow and develop throughout life.

As atoms interact together, so too does our Quantum Self or energy entangle, bond and influence reality through the creation of true and meaningful connections. The stronger those connections become, the deeper the transfer of energy between the two energetic entities. Furthermore, just as we experience different degrees of chemistry when we meet people (sometimes you might like someone straight away, and other times you don't like someone even if you don't have a valid reason), the quality and quantity of said personal entanglement is also affected by these unique connections.

As you reinforce or separate from this Quantum Interpersonal Entanglement, the connection and "chunk" of energy shared and exchanged will also evolve. Similar to the mechanism of neurons and memory, if we continuously reinforce certain connections, they will be more likely to remain in our conscious awareness.

Otherwise, they might end up disappearing and forgotten. Some interpersonal Quantum Entanglements might burst instantly and last a lifetime; others might never be forced to endure no matter how hard we try or could fade rapidly once we lose contact with that person.

This is the basic process for all life forms, at any age, and regardless complexity or the richness of social life. Even an amoeba, requiring a very limited amount of quantum energy to function and live, experiences the basic reactions of attraction and repulsion as it adapts to its environment. The essence that defines life is the same for all species, and they only differ in terms of complexity and execution. This is not limited to Earth, but applies to all corners of our universe, and even to different ways of "being alive".

So you die, your Quantum Self moves into a plane where the rules of Quantum Mechanics apply, you lose most of your consciousness, and whatever was meant by "you". Then what?

10.4. Reincarnation

Having tackled the path of the Quantum Self at the end of life, we need to question the purpose of death

219

and what happens after. Energy cannot be created or destroyed, but it can be transformed. Therefore, it would not make any sense to consider each new life as an immaculate clean sheet that fabricates a new Quantum Self out of the genetic predisposition of the biological body. After all, all the primal quantum energy that enables life in its different forms was generated at the same time as the universe itself – more on that later. This is where the concept of the spiritual recycling, or reincarnation, comes into play.

Reincarnation is commonly known as the rebirth of the aspect of an individual that persists after bodily death in one or more successive existences. Depending on the tradition, these existences may be human, animal, spiritual, or vegetable. While belief in reincarnation is most characteristic of South Asian and East Asian traditions, it also appears in other modern religions and beliefs. However, the major religions that hold a belief in reincarnation arose in India.

In Hinduism, the process of birth and rebirth is endless until one achieves *Moksha*, or liberation (literally "release") from that process. *Moksha* is achieved when one realises that the eternal core of the individual (*Atman*) and the Absolute reality (*Brahman*) are one.

When this occurs one can escape from the cyclical process of death and rebirth (*Samsara*).

The concept of becoming part of a greater source of energy aligns with the claims made by Quantum Psychology. Perhaps, even when we are alive, confined as individual, and restrained within our body, those limits between what is *our energy* and what is *the greater torrent of energy* are not rigid, but interconnected. Indeed, when we entangle or connect with other people we '*give away*' part of our essence or soul, and '*add*' part of other people's spirit to our own.

However, to think that this process holds an ultimate conscious, and somehow '*socially desirable*' purpose, like aiming to 'become one with brahman', seems too tied to the social conventionalisms and macroscopic laws. Because, if that were the case, how would you know "the right thing to do" to bring you closer to that goal? And what would happen after that goal is achieved?

From another perspective, Buddhism denies the existence of an unchanging, substantial soul or self, and holds a belief in the transmigration of the karma that is accumulated by an individual in life. Passing our karma on to the next soul as we leave the reality of this existence.

Although the concept of "dispossession" of one's self might seem interesting and daunting, by embracing the idea of any kind of cosmic judgment (God or karma), we relinquish our most powerful and basic inherited nature. From a social perspective, right and wrong are concepts that evolve with society. The strength to determine the influence of the karma we create, and whatever consequences it has, comes from us, and not from an external force that holds the key to the absolute truth.

Nevertheless, the concept of karma hints to us that the way we interpret life, and how we feel about ourselves, can determine how we will experience the afterlife. Furthermore, karma proposes that what transcends into our next life are the connections and actions we experience while alive, aligning with the assumptions of Quantum Psychology.

From a more modern perspective, different studies show testimonies of children, between the ages of two and six, reporting experiences from a previous life. The manner in which the reincarnated personality has died is yet another differentiating variable to 'remember' your previous life. Those who suffered a violent death seem to be more prone to host those odd memories. This aligns with what was previously said, that the way we die affects the way we move into the next life.

When death happens unexpectedly, a bigger chunk of our energy trespasses to that quantum plane, and if the reincarnation happens before it starts to fade away into the torrent of that quantum energy, then chances are that the newly incarnated soul will remember events of their previous life. This will happen because, once our Quantum Self interacts with the newly formed DNA in the womb, the newly formed brain will start recreating the same neuron synapses to generate those memories from your previous life.

On the other hand, if death happens naturally and slowly (from a physical or mental perspective, where the person has accepted that he/she will pass away soon), then perhaps that fading in the quantum energy starts happening during life. Then, by the time you get to the other side, there is a 'smaller chunk of you' left, since you are already more integrated with the source of energy that connects and created us all.

For instance, Dr Ian Stevenson, former Professor of Psychiatry at the University of Virginia School of

Medicine, dedicated the majority of his career to finding evidence of reincarnation. Dr Stevenson claimed to have found over 3,000 examples of reincarnation during his time. He interviewed three children who claimed to remember aspects of their previous lives. The children made 30-40 statements each regarding memories that they themselves had not experienced, and through verification, he found that up to 92% of the statements were correct. The statements of the subject, taken as a group, were sufficiently specific so that they could not have corresponded to the life of any other person.

The problem with reincarnation as that its explanation is twofold: we have no way to verify it in an objective manner and we have no plausible mechanism to explain how reincarnation might occur. On top of that, there is always the eternal question from the sceptics of reincarnation: "If we reincarnate, how is it possible that the population keeps growing?" Quantum Psychology might cast some light to answer these questions, even if the concept of reincarnation challenges our identity as beings.

First of all, what is our core essence? As previously discussed, it is the sense of self, experienced as constant throughout life. But a moment's reflection reveals that what really remains constant is the feeling of the sense of self itself, not the content of that sense. Am I even remotely the same person I was at five? At fifteen? Last week? A moment ago? In one way, obviously yes.

Something links the "me" that I am right now to the "me" that I was at five. However, if any content in my life remains constant, it's not due to me remembering it, to me consciously holding it in my working memory so that it doesn't fade and I end up forgetting myself. It is because some things remain constant without me having to remember them or even think about them. And it is that sense, which is the elemental structure of our essence, our Quantum Self, which goes beyond our biological limits, and through reincarnation.

For reincarnation to take place, the consciousness or Quantum Self of your previous life must have entered the body of your current one. In esoteric literature, this is known as the transmigration of the spirit or soul. It is said to occur in the womb, perhaps already at conception or shortly afterward, with the beginning of the rhythmic pulses that develop into the heart of the embryo. The spirit or soul of an individual does not necessarily migrate to another individual of the same species or space-time proximity. Parts of our Quantum Self may not reincarnate at all, evolving and fading with the rest of the eternal flow of quantum energy.

Because, once we die, we move into that quantum plane, where the laws of Quantum Mechanics rule the remains of our "soul". However, we are still entangled to this world through the true emotional connections that were made, transcending the limitations of our biology. As we start to *"lose"* our individuality and slip into the stream of that energy that formed us, we enable reincarnation to happen, as long as the following basic principles are present:

- The possibility to harbour life presents itself again: for example, in humans, that would be when a fecund egg is available.

- The type of life to be conceived: animal, vegetal, microscopic, extra-terrestrial or extra-dimensional. Each is slightly different, but based on the same principles, chemical, and energetic reactions to the stimuli (i.e. that fecund egg), which take place to enable this new organism to hold a 'soul', or enough quantum energy to function and thrive.

- Availability of that required energetic source: sometimes the energy chunk that will create the new life will be formed of a totally new and *"mixed"* source of energy coming from the Quantum Realm – such as made up of the parts of us that fade. Other times, especially if it happens while most of our spiritual "chunk" of energy hasn't faded yet, most of what used to be us will be transported into a new life. Often it may be a mixture of both.

It is key to mention that from a qualitative perspective this reincarnation process will not differ between species. However, perhaps from a quantitative perspective, the amount of the basic ingredients required will determine if the new life is an amoeba or an elephant, for example. Moreover, since time and space are no longer a limitation, reincarnation could even happen on a different planet than the one you last lived on, or even a different manifestation life manifestation, perhaps one not carbon-based. Most likely our Quantum Self, before reincarnating, will feel attracted by certain energetic patterns or stimuli, based in the connections we made while alive, that influence into what, when, and where we reincarnate.

Contrarily to the patriarchal and religious approach towards the afterlife, in this view there is no need to live terrified of doing whatever is socially or culturally accepted as 'good', in order to access heaven, or experience a better reincarnation. Right and wrong are not set in stone, and it is ultimately down to you to determine what is right because, well, if it's right, you will feel good about it, which will determine how your Quantum Self will transcends to the next plane.

Ultimately, how our Quantum Self interacts with others in life, influences the way it will interact with that current of eternal energy. Simply put, if we find balance and purpose during life, we will be more attuned with the Quantum Realm by the time we pass, and that transition will, therefore, be more natural and peaceful.

Summarizing, in order to explain those reincarnation memories reported during childhood, it must be that the Quantum Self of that person live on the same planet, was human, and passed into the new body before the soul faded away into the source of quantum energy that populates the universe. The low probability of all those factors occurring would explain why it is not a frequent phenomenon.

This is the way we transcend, becoming beings bigger than our own life. The means and process may vary based on the particularities of each situation, but the basics of how it works remain unaltered amongst people, species or even planets, as we are all made of the same basic energy and ruled by the same laws of physics.

However, some factors may seriously alter this process. For example, radioactivity has a harmful effect on our atomic structure and Quantum energy. Just as happens with our cells, high doses of radioactivity can also corrupt the core of our Quantum Self, annihilating even that essence of ourselves. This would be like shaking a picture made of sand, each grain would lose its place of harmony, resulting in a blur of sediment and dust where are art used to be.

In addition to all the above, on certain occasions, especially if it happens before we totally fade into that torrent of Quantum energy, a big *"chunk"* of our Quantum Self might get split into more than one physical body. A clear example would be the inner connection between twins. While the twin bond is a unique relationship, sometimes it's endowed with extraordinary, seemingly telepathic, qualities. While the phenomenon is assumed to be more common in monozygotic (identical) twins because they share a closer genetic connection, dizygotic, or fraternal twins, aren't excluded.

There is plenty of anecdotal data to support the idea of some sort of twin telepathy. Commonly, twins seem to share an inherent understanding of their co-twins emotional state. Many report a sensation of "something being wrong" when their twin is in crisis. However, there simply isn't any empirical proof of this twin connection at a quantum or extracorporeal level. In cases where twins were raised separately but had similar clothes and tastes when they did meet, the similarities might reflect the genetic component of personality and interests.

Despite the lack of scientific proof, the personal experiences twins share can't be denied. The connection between twins represent a deep and strong Quantum Interpersonal Entanglement that lasts for life and starts in the very same womb, the moment that the quantum energy 'insufflates' into the fecund eggs – especially if they share just one source of quantum energy.

However, environmental and genetic factors will also play a role in these situations, even in explaining some of the similarities of twins separated at birth. But there is more to it, because this phenomenon can also be observed between non-twins in a close relationship, such as a husband and wife who have been married for many years, reinforcing the importance of Quantum Interpersonal Entanglements.

The giving up of part of our so beloved biological identity and individuality could explain the continuous population growth, even within the framework of reincarnation. There is no ultimate greater purpose or search towards unique rightness when thinking about the afterlife, but just a natural process, fired by basic chemical and physic laws; just like an object falls because of gravity, without a bigger and more socially accepted reason behind.

Then, a powerful question echoes from the deepest of the rabbit whole: *if there is no beacon guiding objective right and wrong, what's the meaning of everything?*

CHAPTER 11: THE ORIGIN OF THE UNIVERSE, THE MEANING OF LIFE, GOD AND BEYOND

Having begun to understand the nature of our beings, that which transcends our biological limitations, it is time to locate our true place in the Universe and existence as a whole. To understand why this Universe we live in is the way it is, what the ultimate meaning of life is, and where God fits in amongst all this. It is time for our Quantum Self to speak up and unravel the depths of reality and purpose.

11.1. Why Is the Universe the Way It Is?

It is commonly assumed that life emerged as a consequence of a physical Universe that was created first. Therefore, life spontaneously hatched as an "accident", determined and shaped by the conditions given by the ability of that physical environment to harbour it.

However, Quantum Psychology challenges this basic, and often taken-for-granted, principle. Instead, the Universe exists as a consequence of the life forms in it, and not the other way around. Why? Because without conscious beings existing in the physical world, aware and able to interact with this part of reality, what would be the difference between the Universe existing or not existing in the first place?

Without the power and control of the *"observer"*, the very same observer that changes the way subatomic particles behave, the Universe itself couldn't be conceived as a reality. Without consciousness, there is no possibility for the conception of anything else existing at all. The true nature of the Universe cannot be understood by inspecting spiral galaxies or watching distant supernovas, it lies deeper; it starts from our own selves.

A more accurate understanding of the world requires that we consider it to be biologically centred. It's a simple but amazing concept, which the theory of Biocentrism, introduced by Robert Lanza, attempts to clarify: life creates the Universe, instead of the other way around. This model is driven in part by the on-going attempts to create an overarching view, a theory of everything. Such efforts have now stretched for decades, without much success; however, as has been presented, our Quantum Self can cover that gap, acting as the necessary bridge to articulate all other aspects of reality around it.

When it comes to articulating the origin and composition of the universe, most of the comprehensive theories fail to take into account one crucial factor: we are creating them. It is the biological creature that fashions the stories, that makes the observations, and that gives names to things. And therein lies the great expanse of our oversight, that science has not confronted the one thing that is at once most familiar and most mysterious – consciousness.

The double slit experiment has led to a theory that consciousness collapses the wave functions of anything into its particle state. That means that, without consciousness, everything is just shimmering waves of probability until someone is conscious of it, then it collapses the probabilities into a tangible reality.

What Biocentrism states is that before consciousness, the Universe was just shimmering waves of probability. One of those probabilities created the probability of life, which created consciousness, and consciousness collapsed the Universe's wave state into a physical state. According to Biocentrism, you are a unified being, not just your wriggling arm or foot, but part of a larger equation that includes all the colours, sensations and objects you perceive. If you divorce one side of the equation from the other, you cease to exist. Indeed, experiments confirm that particles only exist with real properties if they are observed. That's why in real experiments, the properties of matter – and space and time themselves – depend on the observer. Your consciousness isn't just part of the equation – the equation is you.

The Universe only exists because of an individual's consciousness of it; the Universe itself does not create life. The same applies to the concepts of space and time. However, following some of the principles proposed by Biocentrism, Quantum Psychology goes further, widening the understanding of the essence and meaning of the Universe and our consciousness.

Historically, the origin of the Universe and the origin of life have been studied assuming that the former started way before the latter. To a certain degree that is true, as life as we know it needs some basic physical conditions to exist. However, from a Quantum Psychology perspective, the essential energy that defines life (the soul, spirit, Quantum Self...), the very same energy that differentiates us from inanimate matter, was created at the same time as the Universe. Therefore, the current of primal quantum energy, which we are both connected to and independent of, hatched at the very same moment that the Universe, and everything in it, came into existence.

But when and why did the Universe begin? How is it possible that everything falls in such delicate and orchestrated balance, and doesn't collapse? The Big Bang Theory (not the TV series I'm afraid) is the most accepted and extended explanation of the origin of the Universe from a scientific perspective. According to the theory, the early Universe was hot and dense. As time passed, the Universe expanded, cooled, and became less dense. The theory of the Big Bang explains why distant galaxies are moving away from us, and why the speed that they move away from us is proportional to distance. It explains why most of the visible Universe is made of hydrogen and helium.

However, modern perspectives are enriching this approach to the origin of the Universe with more complete explanations. The cyclic Universe theory, for example, is a model of cosmic evolution according to which the Universe undergoes endless cycles of expansion and cooling, each beginning with a "big bang" and ending in a "big crunch".

The theory is based on three underlying notions. First, the big bang is not the beginning of space or time, but rather a moment when gravitational energy and other forms of energy are transformed into new matter and radiation and a new period of expansion and cooling begins. Second, the bangs have occurred periodically in the past and will continue periodically in the future. Third, the sequence of events that set the large-scale structure of the Universe that we observe today took place during a long period of slow contraction before the bang.

Although the cyclic model differs radically from the conventional theory of the big bang, both theories match all current observations with the same degree of precision. Nevertheless, none of the theories address one taunting question: why was the Universe created with such a particular disposition and set of laws, and not any other way? For example, a reality where the laws of physics and chemistry are completely different, creating squared planets instead of spherical ones; or where the stars emanate darkness instead of light; or perhaps one endless continuum of solid matter, making it theoretically possible to walk from one corner of the Universe to the other.

The answer can be rather simple and parsimonious: **The reason for the Universe being the way it is, is simply because it can linger this way.** It is natural to think that there is only one possible big bang or big crunch, where everything was beautifully and perfectly created the way we know it on the first try. Call it the power of God to design such balanced perfection, or a consequence of the rigidity of the laws of physics and chemistry, all predictable, predetermined and pre-designed to succeed.

However, imagine, instead, that an immense and chaotic source of energy generated all kind of reactions as a result of its power. Those energetic manifestations (or 'big bangs') would hatch randomly, or as a reaction of the previous one, but would end up collapsing due to a lack of sustainability. Just like if a newly born organism is not physically fit to thrive in its environment, it will perish. Each big bang would represent an exercise of trying and retrying until *"something sticks"*. Sometimes this collapse and reset to square one would occur instantly, sometimes that newly born Universe might begin to exist, just to stop doing so after such balance is found to be unsustainable, breaking and starting the process all over again.

But, eventually, there is a big bang that creates a disposition of the Universe that can actually self-sustain and thrive. Just as in nature, only a Universe where the laws and rules resulting from the 'big bang' of that energy source can persist will be one that actually prevails. In our experience, *our* big bang configuration allowed for everything we know, and what we don't know just yet, to exist without imploding or collapsing.

Does this mean that the Universe as we know is a consequence of a *successful* big bang, instead of a failed one? For all we know and experience, obviously yes. However, when considering this trial-and-error attempt at creation, there is no black and white type of judgement. One Universe might take only a few seconds to collapse due to the impossibility of its disposition to persevere; another can take trillions of years until the *'glitch'*, or consequence of everything else created in that Universe, resets everything, either instantly or over time; there might be another big bang where a Universe is created with no time or space at all!

Therefore, even if *our* Universe and reality is an extremely successful one (as far as we can tell), by definition of eternity, it will not be immovable and perfectly balanced forever; at one point or another, it will reset itself again. Ironically and parallel to human condition, the Universe constantly moves towards that glitch that will break its unique perfection and balance.

Furthermore, we only know the Universe in this persistent configuration. There are probably countless combinations that could sustain and thrive over time, as our reality does. Most likely, there are some that even escape what we can imagine and conceive in terms of life, matter, time or space. Almost certainly, some of them happened before and will happen after our own version of reality ends.

Therefore, the Universe is the way it is *"because it can"*, and everything that came with it enabled it to develop everything else: the physical laws, the conceptions of matter, the creation of time and space, even the different types of energies that were released when everything started, including the form of energy that provides life. Because the key ingredient for the persistence of our Universe is that it was created with the preamble that it would be able to harbour life, as the mandatory observer required for reality to exist in the first place.

Once all the other ingredients were conceived and embraced by the way the Universe deployed, it was only a matter of time, given by the chain of reactions, until that source of energy, which enables life, started to hatch around the Universe. As will be explained later on, this life appeared at the slightest chance it could, and not only as we know it on Earth. Let's say that our way of life is the one that was fit to manifest here, but that given the source of primal quantum energy available, it is not the only possibility to conceive life.

But what is the meaning of life then? Why do all beings come to exist, survive and persist through generations?

11.2. The Meaning of Life

I must warn you: the answer proposed from Quantum Psychology might not be as meaningful and romantic as you would expect. Hell, it even challenges your ego as a being and unique creation. However, please bear in mind that the power that lies within us cannot be suppressed.

Understanding the mechanisms that allow this Universe to exist the way it does, doesn't mean that we lose any bit of our inherent power. Because, remember, if it weren't for life and the quantum energy that makes it possible, nothing else would exist: no Universe, no matter, no time or space, and definitely no "God" or whichever religious or spiritual conception you might have. It is because of each one of us, and any other life form that there is out there, that there is a physical reality too.

We have just covered that, theoretically, unnumbered possibilities of reality could be conceived as a consequence of different big bangs. However, no matter how unintuitive all those possible alternative realities are, in all of them there is only one ingredient that needs to be present in order for any version of the Universe to exist: the very same energetic essence that fills each of us, creating our consciousness, life and everything else. This is the endless current of energy that your Quantum Self is made of. The very same one that we, as individuals that experience life and the world in a unique way, are independent of, and at the same time the very same one to which we will always be linked.

This energy, with which we create the Universe, is the same one that connect us with every other living being or piece of matter. Some connection will be stronger, deeper and purer, and others will be weak or irrelevant. It is our core feelings and passions, the emotions that are automatically and energetically created, before all our social and physical limitations kick in, that determine the strength of the connection. Experiencing something meaningful and entangling with someone is the most direct link between ourselves as living individual beings, and the rest of the current of quantum energy to which we belong.

When it comes to answering what the meaning of life is, from a Quantum Psychology perspective, the answer falls simpler than any deep, complicated explanation. Life exists because the conditions and the ingredients of life are present on Earth. Just as if you have gravity, matter, time, and whatever else you need to create a planet, it will naturally form, so too with life.

As with the rest of energy types that reign over the Universe, the type of energy that enables life is also present everywhere. Then, when given the right conditions, life will appear and pop as a chemical reaction, following a pre-set and established set of laws that were drawn during the creation of the Universe. Because, as I said, life is a condition for the existence of the Universe, in the first place; and, for as long as those basic ingredients remain present, life will continue to exist even in the most unlikely environments and situations. It happened in Mars, although the conditions didn't persist long enough for life to evolve into more complex organisms as it did on Earth.

As for the purpose of life, and why all living beings have an intrinsic motivation to survive and reproduce, once more the answer is simple. It is a mere consequence of natural selection. Imagine a primordial pool, filled with unicellular beings, where some of them develop, through genetic and epigenetic mechanisms, an instinct to run away from adversity and toward what's good for them, and another group that doesn't develop any preference in the matter at all. Which group will be more likely to survive and transmit those genetic and epigenetic codes to the next generation?

This simple principle of survival has been reinforced for millions of years, and its complexity has developed as organisms evolved. The result is that every single living being has inherited a deep willingness to survive. Nowadays, a much more complex concept of survival and reproductive instinct is sustained across different species, cultures or even individuals, built into the foundations of the instinct those primitive amoebas developed. Like the collective unconscious Jung proposed, based on that first test of natural selection.

Simply put, there is a will to survive and thrive, and a meaning for the existence of life, because otherwise life would collapse, as would consciousness, and ultimately the Universe, as we know it, would not persist. Because everything exists only because individuals like you and me, or even a virus, plays its role, willing to survive for as long as possible and harbouring a chunk of that essential quantum energy. We are not a consequence of the Universe unfolding around us, the natural conditions Earth that harbours life, or of evolution and natural selection: everything is a consequence of us existing as conscious beings, the mandatory "*observers*". But, is there something bigger than us as individuals?

11.3. Where Is God?

As previously mentioned, the belief in some sort of spirituality or afterlife is almost ubiquitous across all cultures. Often, those beliefs are tied to a conception of a superior or almighty being or God. Western concepts of God have ranged from the detached transcendent demiurge of Aristotle to the pantheism of Spinoza. In whichever form, much of western thought about God has fallen within some broad form of theism. Theism is the view that there is a God, who created and sustains the Universe and is unlimited with regard to knowledge (omniscience), power (omnipotence), extension (omnipresence), and moral perfection.

The beginnings of religion preceded the first members of our species – *Homo sapiens*. Neanderthals reverently buried their dead with a ritual that seems to show that they anticipated life after death. Neanderthals might even have based this belief on some concept of the supernatural. Once we started to anticipate our personal death, humanity was never the same.

Many theologians and anthropologists feel that our first fully human ancestors initially developed primitive concepts of God in order to lessen their anxiety about the future. Thus began the first religion, Animism. This was, and still is, typically found in hunter-gatherer societies. Having developed self-consciousness in themselves, they may have assumed that the rest of the world was equally self-conscious. They began to believe that the rocks, mountains, rivers, sun, moon, trees, land animals, birds, etc. all contained vital powers, each animated by a spirit. Village chiefs, shamans, and native healers played leadership roles in these religions. Human anxiety dissipated somewhat as our distant ancestors felt more in control of nature. Religion gave them assurance, confidence, and peace of mind.

As society evolved, concepts of God in philosophy were entwined with concepts of God in religion. This is most obvious in figures like Augustine and Aquinas, who sought to bring more rigor and consistency to concepts found in religion. Others, like Leibniz and Hegel, interacted constructively and deeply with religious concepts. Even those like Hume and Nietzsche, who criticized the concept of God, dealt with religious concepts. While Western philosophy has interfaced most obviously with Christianity, Judaism and Islam have had some influence. The orthodox forms of all three religions have embraced theism, though each religion has also yielded a wide array of other views.

Issues related to Western concepts of God include the nature of divine attributes and how they can be known, if or how that knowledge can be communicated, the relation between such knowledge and logic, the nature of divine causality, and the relation between the divine and the human will.

Traditionally speaking, God is presented as a fully conscious, purposeful and even judgmental deity. God is usually assumed to have the capacity to oversee everything, holding the ultimate truth of what is right and wrong in any given situation. On the top of that, the concept of God provides a paternal figure that will be waiting for you after you perish, judging your earthly accomplishments and how fit you are according to his/her standards, then punishing or rewarding you accordingly.

From a classical religious perspective, the main purpose of God is to be the creator of everything and the holder of absolute moral truth. Although the teachings and implications of religions are complex, it is generally accepted that by blindly believing in a God you must be willing to give up your power and control over your life, leaving it in the hands of the so-called God and his/her almighty wisdom.

From a social perspective, the concept of God proves valuable for having a generally accepted set of moral and ethical rules that help us cohabit. It is a way to verbalise the basic rights and wrongs that are already dictated by our instinct or social conventionalisms (do not kill, do not steal, etc.). It helps us to live in community and thrive as a species.

However, the idea of a fully conscious superior being, possessing all the qualities that religion attributes to God, feels both "too human" and "too paternal", as if we needed a higher force to watch over us in order to behave properly. It ultimately narrows our capacity to differentiate right and wrong and act accordingly, without the need of a divine punishment, as if we were children.

Quantum Psychology postulates that the only real power and control that matters in our life resides within each of us, nowhere else. We are the reason for the Universe to exist, which means that YOU are responsible, and a crafter of the Universe itself. However, any traditional concept of God demands part of that control and power to be handed to an external force instead.

From a Quantum Psychology point of view, this is partly right and partly wrong. Firstly, the closest concept to *"God"* would fall far too short of the traditional conceptions of a deity. However, it can be translated as the current of eternal quantum energy that enables life to exist when the minimum conditions are present. From this perspective, *God* can be identified as the energetic current we fade into when we perish; it is also the only required ingredient for any conception of the Universe to persist.

However, this source of energy, or *God* – that we all are both part of and independent from – is not a unified conscious being at all, as presented by religions. It is the source of an elemental and necessary energy, as is gravity for example, without a set or meaningful purpose, or indeed any form of consciousness. This means that we do not need to renounce our power and control, since, as with the Universe, the reason for this *God* or source of energy to exist is because we, as individuals, exist and react to the basic ingredients that enable life in all its forms.

This basic, purposeless, yet indispensable, and energetic version of *God* was conceived as a consequence of *our* big bang, as was gravity, time, space, matter and everything else required for the Universe to prevail and persist. It was never a conscious deity, making cosmic decisions and crafting reality as he/she pleases, deciding how important we as a species are to existence or how we should behave to gain her/his favour.

There was no initial holy purpose at all; it was pure chance, made by countless tries of forms or Universes that didn't have the required ingredients to be sustained. It was all created together, without a conscious purpose, and it all started because we, the observer, and any other form of life that must be out there, gave that purpose to *God* and reality, bringing them into existence as soon as we had the required environmental ingredients to hatch.

Therefore, we are not "puppets" of a superior deity that judges us. We are our own jury, judge and executioners. Even in situations that we have no control over we can still master the power to handle them and learn how they will affect us at a spiritual level. It is not in God that you will find the answers to your riddles, but in yourself. And then, if you are lucky enough, in those around you who hold the very same supreme power that you do.

Because we are all connected and part of the same primal source of quantum energy or *God*; yet, we are all individuals and responsible for our thriving and self-development. It is from that original collectivism that our singularity is developed. Just like planets, light years apart, can be formed by the same basic ingredients and laws and you wouldn't consider them to be the same planet.

If you are a very religious person, you might attribute the power of creation to the grace of God. Even from a Quantum Psychology perspective, your belief might be partly right. As the traditional conception of God can be understood as a connection between your Quantum Self and the Quantum Realm, helping you to overcome whatever challenges lie ahead.

However, if we hold all that power to craft reality, how come the physical world is presented with a sense of continuity and doesn't change to our will? How come, no matter how connected you are to the Quantum Realm, your wallet will not be filled with money tomorrow morning out of nowhere? If, in the quantum world, all possibilities coexist until the present moment catches up and only one can be presented, why do things not randomly change, but instead stay stable in shape and matter?

The answer is simple: when the Universe began, the energies and rules were conceived as part of it, this sense of continuity was a consequence of its sustainability, and the different forces cannot break each other's basic rules. It is true that those forces, the ingredients of the Universe, interact and influence each other (gravity, dark matter, light, time, space, quantum energy); however, if the rules were that observers (or us as individuals) could completely change the physical reality at will, the Universe wouldn't be able to exist.

Simply put, if everyone had the power to win the lottery by altering reality via their conscious quantum energy, reality wouldn't sustain itself, too many people would win that lottery whether they had the winning combination or not. Therefore, as a consequence of that try and retry sequence of big bangs until a self-sustained universe emerged. The continuity of time-space that we experience are required for the rest of the ingredients to fall into place.

If you should absorb one idea, let it be this: do not underestimate your own power and domain over absolutely everything that exists, even in the situations where you cannot be fully aware or perceive all the factors involved. Because Quantum Psychology is a story about time, space and profound interpersonal connections, and how, for far too long, we have taken those three concepts for granted. Because our biology is deceiving, even when the alternatives are presented right in front of us; there is a part of you, that is as real as your body, that interacts with, and is part of, this quantum plane of existence.

And, through what happens on that plane, we create the reality of our time-space continuum and how it is deployed to us. The Quantum Self, and its source of energy, is the origin, the absolute centre of existence that enables everything else to exist in the first place. Without that crucial ingredient, all the rest that constitutes the Universe would be pointless.

The only factor any conception of existence cannot forego is that the very core essence, quantum energy, connects us all and, at the same time, makes us individually unique. In essence, *you*, and the connections you make, are the reason for everything to exist.

Therefore, you will never be wrong when fighting and following that intrinsic instinct of connecting with someone for whom you care, no matter how crazy your real goal seems to everyone else.

CHAPTER 12: RE-THINKING THE PERCEPTION AND STUDY OF SPACE AND TIME

As mentioned before, this is a story about space, time and profound interpersonal connections, and how the three of them can be deceiving if taken from our limited social and biological perspective. However, as we have already seen, the whole Universe is determined and only has a sense of purpose for as long as consciousness exists to interact with it. Therefore, the study of the concepts of time and space should shift from being physics-centric to a consciousness-centric; this is the perspective that Quantum Psychology proposes.

However, historically the most robust sciences have tackled the study of time and space from a purely physical and tangible perspective, omitting from the equation one crucial ingredient: the required observer. This has allowed for accurate description and prediction of some of the characteristics and phenomena occurring in reality, but mystery, uncertainty, and loopholes, still remain. Many have given up, arguing that there are some questions that can never be answered. Nevertheless, if humankind had always taken that approach, we would still be living in caves.

In this chapter we will cover a holistic and inclusive perspective, beyond the traditional scientific perspective, to understand why our conceptions of time and space can be misleading, incomplete and sometimes, senseless.

12.1. The 'Infinite' Universe

Many cosmologists now think our spatial Universe is infinite. Note that I'm not talking about the "parallel universes" theory here, but the consideration of our space, in the physical reality we perceive, as *never-ending*. As we already covered, scientific evidence points out that the Universe began 13.8 billion years ago with the Big Bang. The Universe has been expanding and cooling ever since, up to and including the present day.

That same theory postulates that eventually, our Universe will run out of momentum and collapse back into a Big Crunch. As so the story will repeat itself over and over again cyclically.

If you have given any thoughts to the idea of infinity, you might say something like: "So, okay, maybe we're in a vast infinite space, but it's mostly empty. Our Universe is just a finite number of galaxies rushing away from each other inside this empty infinite space – like a solitary skyrocket exploding and sending out a doomed shower of sparks."

But many cosmologists would disagree; as far as experts can tell, there are an infinite number of galaxies in our infinite space. The simplest cosmology that fits the assumptions of the large-scale characteristics of the Universe is the so-called Friedmann-Lemaître-Robertson-Walker cosmology, describing a space-time that is homogeneous (the same everywhere) and isotropic (has no preferred direction). Therefore, from this perspective, the universe may be expanding in time, with geometry of space that is Euclidean. The simplest topology that corresponds to Euclidean geometry (the classic blackboard geometry of high school) is that of flat, infinite space. So, by Occam's razor, i.e., the parsimony of assumptions (the simplest explanation is likely to be correct), we can conclude that in the absence of evidence to the contrary, the Universe appears infinite.

On the contrary, Einstein's general theory of relativity proposed a finite Universe with a non-Euclidean space. Astronomers such as de Sitter were uncomfortable with this idea. De Sitter suggested an infinite Universe to make Relativity and Euclidean space compatible, requiring that matter move apart from each other. Indeed, Hubble was able to determine that galaxies are moving away from us, following on from his determination of the distance to the Andromeda galaxy, and the realisation that Andromeda was composed of stars similar to those in the Milky Way. If the galaxies are moving away from each other, it makes sense that they started from an original point – a.k.a. the Big Bang – a conclusion Lemaître came to in 1931.

As you can see, science gives inconclusive perspectives as to whether the Universe is finite or infinite. Perhaps, we need to challenge that reality and the boundaries beyond the biological perception of reality we are accustomed to. What if time and space could be conceived as an integrated dimension, differently to how we traditionally conceive it? Since our default sensory system and perception was designed to survive on your immediate environment on Earth, we would need a broader and more abstract approach to fully comprehend how space is arranged.

From a Quantum Psychology perspective, we would need to take into consideration the essence of our existence, our Quantum Self, leaving aside everything else that we experience. From this perspective, it will be possible to see the real depths of the planes of reality. Just as a fish living in the deepest of the ocean is usually blind, we are biologically blind to comprehend the nature of the Universe from this perspective.

In order for us to be able to fully understand the spatial limits of the Universe and what may lay beyond its plenitude, we will need to think outside the box, to bend and turn all the rules we know here on Earth, to assume things that will just not make any sense if stick with reality just as it *appears* to be. It will only be when we are able to make that 'creative leap', that we will discover that the origin, size, and movement, of all the galaxies are qualitative and quantitatively different to our intuition.

However, one thing does seem clear: assuming that the Universe is infinite seems absurd. But let's imagine, for a moment, that the Universe is indeed infinite. Then, if we assume that there are a finite number of ways that matter can occur (i.e. the way a planet is, or how many ways your favourite cereal box can be designed), it would mean that, in an infinite Universe, the configurations of matter would, eventually, be repeated. Therefore, there would be an infinite number of galaxies and planets. And, since we are assuming that space will never end, eventually we would find another Solar System that is just like ours, but maybe with sustainable variations (for example, a planet Earth where your favourite cereal box has a different design). However, if we continue going further and further – again, with no spatial limitations – we will end up finding an infinite number of *Earth* doppelgangers. Eventually, one of them would be exactly the same as *our Earth*. And, as we continue our journey through infinity, we will repeatedly find replicas of Earth, an infinite number of times. Furthermore, in all of them, your favourite cereal box will also be designed the exact same way.

This concept might be overwhelming; but, in reality, it is just nonsense to think that there are infinite copies of us in this Universe, doing exactly the same thing you are doing now, just far away in space. Quantum Psychology instead proposes that our consciousness is the central energy, articulating everything else around it, and assumes that our elemental individuality, our Quantum Self, cannot be replicated.

So, how is it then? Well, to be honest, there is no solid answer to that. Understanding it would require a level of perception that is too far away from our own. Like trying to explain to an ant that the world is divided in continents and oceans.

However, once we embrace our inherent importance within the realms of reality, we will be able to find truly relevant conclusions about the extent and frontiers of the Universe, realising that it was never a question of measurable size, but an answer of qualitative and flexible composure, all along. But, how much can our consciousness influence spatial reality?

12.2. What Is Our Reach of Influence in the Universe?

We have already covered the power we all contain within ourselves to influence and shape the reality around us, through our Quantum Self and the connection with the Quantum Realm. However, how far can we exercise such influence in the Universe? Is it some sort of butterfly effect, where our consciousness and energy affect what's happening on the other side of the world?

Considering how the mere presence of an observer influences the way subatomic particles behave, bending the limitations of space and time as we understand them, it could be plausible that the energy we project into the world as conscious observers would have repercussions anywhere and anytime. However systematic reality may be, it is much more complex than that. Taking that conclusion blindly would mean ignoring three key considerations of how Quantum Psychology works.

Firstly, there is entanglement. The way we can influence how reality is shaped is tied up with how we can entangle with our environment at a quantum level. Therefore, the reach of our direct influence will be limited to those spaces and times encapsulated within our body's limits and biological existence – hence why your energy cannot influence someone unknown to you, living in a totally different space or time than you.

For our Quantum Self to be able to have an impact in some reality, we need to have interacted and entangled with it. Then, we would open up a channel, which, at the same time, also retro influences us. And, as proposed by Quantum Psychology, the degree of your self-awareness in the situation would depend on your individual characteristics and ability for such perceptions.

Secondly, we cannot ignore the power within ourselves. Every conscious organism has a unique biological, spiritual and quantum set up, which will have weight in any outcome. Therefore, the reach of your energy is partly determined by yourself: where you are focusing and targeting such energy, your patterns of behaviour (whether adaptive or dysfunctional), the connections you make, your mind-set, and your ability and strength to project that energy. An enormous number of dynamic individual factors, all coming from within ourselves, determine how much of an impact we can have in shaping the events of reality.

Finally, it must be remembered that the elemental forces that shape and give sustainability to the Universe cannot violate each other. That means that, regardless of how much we train our Quantum Self, our biological bodies will never be able to break the force and rules of gravity. Our biological and social being also belongs to a world with forces tied up to different principles than our essential energy does. Complimentarily, the laws and principles of our physical world will never be able to suppress those forces coming from our Quantum Self: the ones where time, space and interpersonal connections happen beyond the limitations of our biological perception.

And, as we continue to explore and further understand the potential of Quantum Psychology, we will also be able to expand our reach and influence over the rest of the Universe. We will be able to leave the limitations given by our assumptions of time and space. However, once we master the potential of our Quantum Self, will we be able to fully travel through time at our will, as subatomic particles do?

12.3. The Impossibility of Time-Travelling to the Past

Have you ever dreamt about travelling to the past to change something you deeply regret? Or interfere in a major historic event? Although the idea may be appealing, once you pull that thread, it soon leads to a dead end, unable to answer a very simple question: if time travel to the past were possible, how come we don't know of any time-travellers?

It would seem that time travelling to the past is just not possible at our biological scale. Mostly because we would need to break the other forces of nature that reign over our biological reality. And, as previously mentioned, not even in the plane of our Quantum Self can the rules of the other forces of the universe be broken.

However, in the double slit experiment, particles did travel into the past when forced to take one of the openings. Similarly, the part of our consciousness ruled by quantum laws is able to bend time and space once the social and biological limitations are left behind, as we saw in the Quantum Psychology explanation of the afterlife. It is also true that a part of our Quantum Self or soul stays anchored and connected in those moments, places, and people, that bring deep meaning to our biological existence, remaining as a beacon and allowing our consciousness to return to in a moment of need, whether biologically alive or dead.

Nevertheless, from the plane of existence of our biological and physical self, the closest experience we have of travelling into the past comes from observing the stars in the sky. For example, the Milky Way galaxy is roughly 100,000 light-years wide, so light from its more distant stars can take thousands upon thousands of years to reach Earth. Observe that light, and you're essentially looking back in time.

There's nothing in Einstein's theories or any other robust explanation that precludes time travel into the past. However, the very premise of pushing a button and going back to yesterday violates the law of causality, or cause and effect. One event happens in our Universe, and it leads to yet another in an endless one-way string of events. In every instance, the cause occurs before the effect. Just try to imagine a different reality, say, in which a murder victim dies of his or her gunshot wound before being shot. It violates reality, as we know it; thus time travel to the past must be an impossibility.

However, astrophysics gives us one possible pathway: one could possibly harness the power of a black hole to venture through time and space. How would that work? According to general relativity, a rotating black hole could create a wormhole – a theoretical link between two points of space-time, or perhaps even two points in different universes. However, there's a problem with black holes. They have long been thought to be unstable and therefore un-traversable. However, recent advances in physics theories have shown that these constructs could, in fact, provide a means of travelling through time.

So, what would happen if, somehow, someone managed to go through a wormhole and not die in the process, and yet manage to travel back to the past? Well, most likely the person would create a parallel universe where his/her actions wouldn't affect the space-time reality of the universe he/she left behind, like a new storyline that will develop independently of the original one. Therefore, even in this case, in the timeline of the original reality, we would never be able to perceive or benefit from any changes our wormhole time-traveller had made.

At its best, travelling to the past could only be of use to the traveller to change aspects of his/her life. Yet, what use would it have to change something that happened to me as a child and stay in that reality until I am as old as I am now? Or to live in the Roman Empire where whatever change I implement, I will never get to see its impact on the future, as I will die in that ancient time anyway? Time travelling to the past not only seems unfeasible, but also pointless. However, there is another type of time travel that is not only possible, but also necessary for as to thrive as species: let's go to the future.

12.4. Time-Travelling into the Future

When it comes to time travel into the future, the perspective is totally different than going back in time. Unfortunately, no one has any control over how quickly that time passes, and nobody can stop time and continue to live. It seems that time is a one-way street, always moving forward, it's just a question of how fast the trip will be.

The faster you move through space, the slower you will move through time. We have been able to measure this with ultra-precise atomic clocks in jet airplanes, and the precision offered by the GPS system takes this into account. Some scientists have proposed the idea of using faster-than-light travel to journey forward in time. According to Special Relativity, when you move through space-time, close to the speed of light, time goes slower for you than for the people you left behind, but you won't notice this effect until you return to those stationary people.

Say you were 15 years old when you left Earth in a spacecraft travelling at about 99.5% of the speed of light (which is much faster than we can achieve now) and celebrated only five birthdays during your space voyage.

When you get home at the age of 20, you would find that all your classmates were 65 years old, retired, and enjoying their grandchildren! Because time passed more slowly for you, you will have experienced only five years of life, while your classmates will have experienced a full 50 years.

Now, you might claim that this is not time travel; it's age retardation at best. It doesn't matter that, due to your accelerated reference frame, it seems to only be, say 5 years. From a viewpoint outside that accelerated reference frame, you were gone 50 years. Moreover, and according to the principles of Quantum Psychology, it is our subjective perception and consciousness what makes the perception of this situation forward time travel. It is our observation, linked to the biological and physical forces we interact with, that frames and gives meaning to that relativity with time and space.

One of those forces interacting with our Quantum Self, and affecting time and space, is gravity. According to Einstein's theory of general relativity, gravity can bend time. If you want to advance through the years a little faster than the next person, you'll need to exploit space-time. Global positioning satellites pull this off every day, accruing an extra third-of-a-billionth of a second daily.

Time passes faster in orbit, because satellites are farther away from the mass of the Earth. Down here on the surface, the planet's mass drags on time and slows it down in small measures. We call this effect gravitational time dilation.

The movie *Interstellar* shows a planet orbiting very close to a black hole. In the movie, one hour spent on the planet has the people back on Earth ageing seven years because of the gravity of said black hole. The film also hints about the importance of our raw emotions and personal connections in shaping the Universe, influencing the way time and space deploy. Our consciousness is so deterministic upon the physical world that it has the ability to bend time and space at its will, similar to how gravity or speed do. And, as Quantum Psychology proposes, amongst all the feelings that we can harbour, love is the strongest, purest and most entangling one of them all. But we will cover more of that in Chapter 14.

12.5. The Subjective Perception of Time & Space

Generally speaking, the perception of time refers to a person's subjective experience of the passage of time, or the perceived duration of events, which can differ significantly between individuals, species and/or in different circumstances. Although physical time appears to be objective (with the exceptions we just covered), psychological time is subjective and potentially malleable, exemplified by common phrases like "time flies when you are having fun" and "a watched pot never boils". This malleability is made particularly apparent by the various temporal illusions we experience.

Time, as easily measurable and quantifiable as it is, is not free from the power of subjective variation. We take for granted the singularity of this reality, even if it shows a clear proof that the way we experience and interact with the Universe is not linear, where our consciousness plays a key role in how this reality is unveiled to us.

Furthermore, research shows that the perception of time has a huge inter-species variation. As a general rule of thumb, time seems to pass more slowly for lighter animals with faster metabolisms. In fact, for a fly the world seems to move approximately seven times slower than it seems to for humans, while the leatherback sea turtle perceives time at a rate that is around two and a half times faster than a human. Therefore, flies avoid being swatted in just the same way Keanu Reeves dodges flying bullets in the movie The Matrix – by watching time pass slowly.

In evolutionary terms, the ability to perceive time on very small scales may be the difference between life and death for small, vulnerable animals. These findings show that differences in how a mouse and an elephant sense time are not arbitrary but rather are finely tuned by interactions with their surroundings.

We do not so much perceive time itself, but changes in, or the passage of, time, or what might be described as "events in time". In particular, we are aware of the temporal relations between events, and we perceive events as being either simultaneous or successive. We also have a perception of the sequence or order of these events.

But, how do we perceive time? Although psychologists believe that there is a neurological system governing the perception of time, it appears not to be associated with specific sensory pathways, but rather uses a highly distributed system in the brain. Time perception therefore differs from our other senses – sight, hearing, taste, smell, touch, even proprioception – since time cannot be directly perceived, and so must be "reconstructed" in some way by the brain.

When the brain receives new information from the outside world, the raw data does not necessarily arrive in the order needed to process it properly. The brain therefore reorganises the information and presents it in a more easily understandable form. In the case of familiar information, very little time is needed for this process, but new information requires more processing and this extra processing tends to make time feel elongated. This is part of the reason why a child's summer seems to last forever, while an old person's well-practiced routine seems to slip away faster and faster. The more familiar the task, the less new information the brain needs to process, and the more quickly time seems to pass.

Also, to some extent, the perception of time is associated with other cognitive processes such as attention. Measuring the duration of an event requires a certain amount of attention, and new events appear to take longer than familiar events because more attention is paid to them. For instance, in psychological tests, if the same picture is shown again and again, interspersed every so often with a different picture, the different picture is perceived by the observer as staying on-screen for longer, even if all the pictures actually appear for the same length of time. The difference arises from the degree of attention paid to the pictures.

There is not enough evidence to explain the underlying mechanisms leading to why we perceive time as subjectively variable, even if from a physical perspective it is constant and linear. However, even if there is something we experience constantly, scientific research seems to have ignored the supremacy of our own subjective perception of time over the easily measurable physical time.

It is true that the time we have is limited, and nothing is more valuable from a biological perspective than the amount of it that we have left. Therefore, understanding how our own consciousness is able to shape and control the way time elapses for us shows the importance of our own power over the physical world around us. This assumption challenges the way we believe time and space work, where we are "victims", or a consequence, of them, when it really is the other way around, as Quantum Psychology implies.

To date, the way we study the implications of space and time in the Universe have been too biologically focused. From this perspective, our perception of time was designed exclusively to make us survive on Earth for a certain number of years. Therefore, in order to fully understand the scope of the time-space continuum, we require two things: thinking about new and creative ways to measure and perceive space and time; and acknowledging the importance of our own mind into shaping the way the space-time continuum unfolds, as the bridge that articulates everything else within the universe.

CHAPTER 13: FUTURE APPLICATIONS OF QUANTUM PSYCHOLOGY

So far, we have covered the implications of how our Quantum Self interacts and influences the way reality unfolds, filtered by that part of our consciousness. However, we haven't yet addressed the extent of the impact Quantum Physics and Quantum Psychology could have in different aspects of our society. As we will see in this chapter, the future applications, resulting from digging into the Quantum Realm, will change the way we live, communicate, and even our limits as a species.

Almost every aspect of our life will be modulated or influenced by this new way of understanding our human experience and the Universe. And, as the theory and implications grow, the importance of our consciousness in shaping and changing the macroscopic world will become clear. Please bear in mind that, for most of the upcoming topics, it may take centuries before they become common reality; however, for other aspects we are already starting to sense the path that will lead us to the coming of advances.

13.1. Technology

Within the advances and possibilities of Quantum Mechanics, the technological side is more developed than the other topics I will cover. You probably have already heard about quantum computers, which are expected to be the future of our own PC's in about two decades.

To get to grips with quantum computing, first remember that an ordinary computer works on 0s and 1s, as designed by Alan Turing in the 1930s. However clever an algorithm might appear, all it ever does is manipulate strings of *bits* – where each bit is either a 0 or a 1.

Quantum computing is based on the fact that, in the quantum world, things don't have to be as clear-cut as we'd expect from our macroscopic experience. As you know, tiny particles, such as electrons or photons, can take on simultaneous *states,* that we would normally deem mutually exclusive, in what we call superposition – like how an atom can act as a particle or a wave. A quantum computer, rather than representing *bits,* uses *qubits*, which can take on the value 0, or 1, or both simultaneously. This parallelism allows a quantum computer to work on a million computations at once, while your desktop computer works on one.

But there is more to quantum physics than superposition. If you look at a system of more than one qubit, then the individual components aren't generally independent of each other. Instead, they can be *entangled,* just like atoms, or we, do. When you measure one of the qubits in an entangled system of two qubits, for example, then the outcome – whether you see a 0 or a 1 – immediately tells you what you will see when you measure the other qubit.

Entanglement means that describing a system of several qubits using ordinary classical information, such as bits or numbers, isn't simply about stringing together the descriptions of the individual qubits. Instead, you need to describe all the *correlations* between the different qubits. As you increase the number of qubits, the number of those correlations grows exponentially: to describe a system of 300 qubits you would already need more numbers than there are atoms in the visible Universe.

The idea is that, since you can't hope to write down the information contained in a system of just a few hundred qubits using classical bits, perhaps a computer running on qubits, rather than classical bits, can perform tasks a classical computer can never hope to achieve. Researchers are also excited about the prospect of using quantum computers to model complicated chemical reactions, a task that conventional supercomputers aren't very good at all.

However, quantum computing faces a massive challenge that impedes the development of its full potential, called quantum decoherence. Quantum decoherence refers to how the qubits lose their quantum status and turn into a normal bit system due to their contact and interaction with the environment, especially when a conscious observer is involved – in other words, any one of us. Due to decoherence, the ability of quantum computers to stay in superposition and/or entangle is severely jeopardised. The larger the system, the bigger the chance that environment will impact the quantum reality of the computer, causing errors and a loss of information. Coherence length is the time a qubit can survive its quantum properties.

Despite this, it is still easy to foresee the huge potential quantum computers can bring into our society in the form of technology. Once we master it, we will be able to apply its principles to any kind of electronic device to enhance its power, speed, and capacity, such as: mobile phones, televisions, kitchen equipment, all types of vehicles, to name a few.

Moreover, Quantum Psychology will take us one step forward along that path. We will start to become aware of our own conscious ability to entangle and influence the outcome of the subatomic particles in the Quantum Realm. Following the effect, the observer has over the behaviour in particles we will be able to extend more properties from Quantum Mechanics into our physical reality.

Eventually, the electronic devices will also be entangled with us. Imagine a mobile phone where all you need to do is think about calling someone, and then the phone makes that call; or a car where you can set the GPS and autopilot just by thinking about your destination. Security systems will also benefit from our quantum awakening, where you will be able to open a safe box if the safe recognises your entangled consciousness.

Every part of our interpersonal communication will be affected by the advances achieved through Quantum Mechanics: we will be able to transmit messages anywhere in the Universe, at any time, using more than just words or body language, but also quantum messages that will be channelled by our own energy and gut sensations. Instead of telling someone we feel happy, we will be able to transport that feeling from our mind into theirs, which will ease and enhance human communication across cultures, and eventually solve or prevent international conflicts.

Furthermore, your electrical equipment will become some sort of extension of yourself, evolving and adapting to your personal preferences, and most likely integrated inside your body. Entangled with them, you will create an intimate connection with this technology, where to find the answer to anything throughout your life, all you will need to do is to think the question.

13.2. The World of Entertainment

Following the technology behind quantum computing, the way we experience entertainment will benefit from the potential of the Quantum Realm.

Let's follow the comparison between a classic computer and a quantum one. As we saw, while the classic one can only compute a limited number of outcomes based on 0s and 1s, a quantum computer can work out all the potential outcomes simultaneously. Likewise, we have already seen in books, videogames or even some pioneering TV series, where our choice can affect and shape where the story goes. If you apply the quantum principles into those formats, then you will, as a result, have a virtually infinite number of possibilities that a story can lead to, based on our choices as an observer.

For instance, we will be able to develop video games, run by quantum computers, where every choice we make will affect the storyline of the game plot. Each game will increasingly become an individualised experience, where augmented reality will also allow us to feel as though we have lived different lives within our own. We will be whoever we choose to be, and as we entangle ourselves with this technology, and the personalisation and experience will only be reinforced.

Similarly, we will have electronic books, movies and TV series where we will be able to shape the stories as they go. From this perspective, writers and directors will still have creative power, giving us the frame of the story and the main characters, from there, how that story unfolds will be up to us. Perhaps some movies, through augmented reality, will even allow us to play a part in the movie, as if we were another actor.

In the future of entertainment we the audience, viewer, and consumer, will take a central and active role in. And, as we discover more and more about the potential of Quantum Psychology, that power, and the number of alternatives, will grow exponentially.

13.3. Teleportation

As we saw on Chapter 5, basic teleportation of subatomic entangled particles is a reality. Do you remember that team in Tenerife that managed to teleport a particle for over 100 kilometres onto another island by entangling it to two atoms allocated in each one of the islands?

Generally speaking, quantum teleportation is a process by which quantum information can be transmitted from one location to another, with the help of classical communication and quantum entanglement between the sending and receiving particles. However, nowadays the limit of the speed of light stands still as a limitation to taking teleportation to a macroscopic level. Nevertheless, this will not always be the case, and eventually we will be able to crack this riddle, which will open the doors to physical teleportation and all its possibilities.

Of course, we have to be careful about what exactly we mean when we say "teleportation". There are three different kinds of teleportation: teleportation through a wormhole (as in Stargate or Interstellar movies), where your body is simply relocated to another place; the Star Trek kind where your molecules are disassembled, beamed somewhere else, and reassembled in the same way (possible through Quantum Entanglement); or the translation of one's person into data to be transmitted, then reconverted into matter, like some organic fax machine. In this chapter we are talking about the last two, since they seem more feasible and controllable than finding or building wormholes that we can survive going through.

It's only a matter of making an observation of the object you want to teleport, which sends that information to the other entangled particle elsewhere. Just like that, your object is teleported, assuming you have enough raw materials on the other side. Of course, teleporting large objects, or people, will probably not happen anytime soon. Keeping particles entangled for a long period of time, over long distances, or along with objects larger than a few particles is way beyond what current technology is capable of.

The day we discover and master how particles can travel faster than the speed of light, bending time and space as they do, will be the day we open the door to creating devices which will allow us to cover vast distances in the blink of an eye. Imagine you are going on a holiday to the other side of the world; you will no longer need to spend long hours queuing in an airport. Instead, there will be some sort of quantum cabins, which will be able to decode our particle composition, and use Quantum Entanglement to recreate it in the desired destination.

Therefore, we will be able to travel anywhere once the technology is implemented. Eventually, this form of teleportation will become cheap and portable, allowing each one of us to have our own teleportation device. When this happens, transport vehicles will be redundant. Then, we will be able to travel and colonize other worlds without the limitations of distance and time. But, how do we first reach those worlds?

13.4. Exploring Other Worlds

The main problems we face in exploring other worlds is the vast distances that need to be covered, the time it takes, and the amount of fuel and supplies required to maintain the crew. Even to travel to our neighbouring planet Mars is deemed an engineering challenge with prohibitive costs. However, when we reveal how subatomic particles travel faster than the speed of light, we will design spaceships that will be able to cover enormous distances of space in the blink of an eye.

Nevertheless, this will be much more complicated than it sounds. Firstly, we will need to make sure that our bodies are designed to travel at that speed without decomposing. Secondly, we will need to understand whether we will need to know beforehand what obstacles might be in our way – for example, not colliding with a small and random comet that would destroy the ship.

Additionally, we would need to know if the conditions of this planet are fit for landing and able to sustain life. Perhaps a non-crewed ship could be sent first to make the required tests. Once those hurdles are overcome, we will be in the position to truly become an intergalactic species. If you add the potential to analyse information mastered by quantum computers, we will be able to map the whole Universe with an exquisite level of detail.

At the same time, connecting our Quantum Self, and aligning with the available quantum technology, we will be in a position to conquer not only the planets suitable for our way of life, but also those where we might not be fit to live, but perhaps other life forms are.

13.5. Extra-terrestrial Life

For centuries humankind has wondered if we are alone in the Universe. Science Fiction has widely covered the idea of other life forms visiting us; however, most of the time, these stories involve conflict and war. This bellicose position comes from our primary instinct to confront any species that challenges our supremacy; just as thousands of years ago we would be wary of people coming from a village far away from ours.

There are many theories out there claiming that we encountered aliens decades, or even centuries (if you believe the pyramids were built by Martians, for example) ago. However, from a Quantum Psychology perspective, this is both true and false.

When conceiving life in other planets there are two dimensions to take into consideration: their level of intelligence, and their plane of existence. From those two factors, we can draw four different possibilities: whether the extra-terrestrial species has already visited us, but remains in secret, or whether we would be able to perceive them with our sensory system or not.

Probability wise, one of the options falls very short, which oddly enough is probably the most accepted one: we are or have already been visited by aliens whose life form is equivalent to ours at a functional and dimensional level. It is hard to assume that if intelligent enough aliens had the technology to travel to Earth, they would choose to observe us in silence and remain hidden. On the other hand, it is also clear that, in the vast Universe, there must be more forms of life, whether they are intelligent or developed enough to make contact with us.

To add more spice into the interspecies communication mix, we need to consider whether we would be able to perceive them and communicate with them anyway. Take for instance a form of life based on in quantum plane, experiencing time and space in a totally different way to us. From their perception of reality, life and subatomic particles bend together in perfect harmony. They wouldn't even need a spaceship to travel through time or space. Technically, they could shape and change our space-time continuum without us even being aware of what's happening, and we wouldn't be able to physically perceive those beings.

Therefore, we wouldn't know that we were interacting with extra-terrestrial entities. Perhaps we have been in touch with galactic beings, they may even influence our life (as in chapter 2, 'the world of the blinds and the deafs'), and we just don't have the capacity or the technology to grasp their message.

We only conceive life as it's given to us under the conditions of Earth. However, it is logical to think that, as conditions change, so will the possible life forms. If we, as a species, want to be ready as to comprehend our place in the Universe, and to reach frontiers of other civilizations, we will have to challenge everything we know about life itself, starting from with our selves.

This is where Quantum Psychology, and the deeper understanding of Quantum Mechanics in general, will allow us to further foresee the possible alternatives and ways to conduct satisfactory communications with other life forms. And, as those beings most likely develop on a different dimensional plane to us, by comprehending how our (sub) consciousness is partly entangled and retro-influenced by the Quantum Realm, we will be led down a path that will take us to new interpretations of our existence on a different level.

13.6. Quantum Chemistry & Biology

A long time ago, before the scientific instrumentation we have today, scientists thought that the atom was the simplest form of matter. However, as time went on, it turned out that they were wrong. There seem to exist particles that actually make up atoms, called subatomic particles. The field of quantum chemistry emerged when this discovery was made, and there were three very important subatomic particles that were found to make up every single atom: protons, neutrons and electrons.

Quantum mechanical models and methods are used to understand matter at its most fundamental level. Quantum chemistry is a branch of chemistry whose primary focus is the application of quantum mechanics in physical models and experiments of chemical systems or molecules.

Quantum chemical methods can often supply predictions of the properties of molecules with great accuracy. But, the more accurate you want to be, the more costly the computation. The special properties of quantum computers should make them ideal for accurately modelling chemical systems. However, so far it has only been feasible to use fully quantum mechanical calculations for molecules with a few atoms. If you want to simulate an entire protein, you need cruder methods such as molecular dynamics, which are based on Newtonian mechanics and at best just build-in quantum effects in a rough, exploratory manner.

Currently, computational drug design is one of the most representative applications of computational chemistry, as thousands of compounds can be easily and quickly screened for compatibility in terms of structure and energetics. Similarly, the vast configuration space of material structure and properties can be explored through simulations that take us closer to the building of functional devices from the bottom up. For example, the design of electrolytes for next generation batteries, the identification of biomaterials for energy storage and separation applications, or the characterisation of optimal structures for organic and hybrid solar cells.

As quantum computers evolve, gaining power and computational capacity, they will be able to simulate increasingly complex chemical molecules, eventually even developing full protein chains, or large networks of different molecules. This will allow us a better understanding of how matter, either biological or not, originated and is formed. Discovering the chemical path that led to the first forms of life will help us to comprehend the complexity of animals as they are today.

Further down the line, as the models of prediction in Quantum Chemistry improve, backed up by the increasing power of quantum computers, we will be able to design life forms that will re-define the rules of life based on DNA and RNA. This new vision, or what will be known as Quantum Biology, will open our eyes and imagination to begin to conceive the different ways life could be represented in the Universe.

Furthermore, as Quantum Psychology also evolves and becomes part of society and daily life, we will be able to measure and accurately describe the type and nature of Quantum connection that a particular species, or individual, has with the Quantum Realm. As our understanding of other species, and life itself, grows so will our ability to protect wildlife and nature. Because, eventually, we will have tangible proof that we all are connected, and that the factors converging the similarities between living beings are far greater than those that divide us.

13.7. Molecular Biology & Quantum Medicine

As Quantum Chemistry gives us new insights into the nature of the molecules that form life, the conclusions will be also applied to common medicine. In fact, there is already a science that is working towards this: molecular biology. However, the step into an even smaller scale is has not yet been taken, the step that will lead us to Quantum Medicine, and all it has to offer.

Molecular biology is the study of biology at a molecular level. The field overlaps with other areas of biology and chemistry, particularly genetics and biochemistry. Molecular biology chiefly concerns itself with understanding the interactions between the various systems of a cell; including the interrelationship of DNA, RNA and protein synthesis, and learning how these interactions are regulated.

While traditional biology concentrated on studying whole living organisms and how they interact within populations (a "top down" approach), molecular biology strives to understand living things by examining the components that make them up (a "bottom up" approach).

Molecules, which form the basis of life, provide scientists with a more predictable and mechanistic tool for scientists to study. Working with whole organisms (or even just whole cells) can be unpredictable, with the outcome of experiments relying on the interaction of thousands of molecular pathways and external factors. Molecular biology provides scientists with a toolkit with which they may "tinker" with the way life works. They may use them to determine the function of single genes or proteins, and to find out what would happen if a particular gene or protein were absent or faulty. Molecular biology is also used to examine when and why certain genes are switched "on" or "off".

The application of principles of molecular biology to treat disease or modify organisms for commercial purposes is generally referred to as genetic engineering. Advances in the fields of molecular biology and genetic engineering are beginning to directly impact clinicians in disease prevention, diagnosis, and treatment. Therefore, an understanding of molecular biology is rapidly becoming necessary to fully understand normal physiology and pathophysiology.

Molecular biology methods have tremendous value, not only in the investigation of basic scientific questions, but also in application to a wide variety of problems affecting the overall human condition. Disease prevention and treatment, generation of new protein products, and manipulation of plants and animals for desired phenotypic traits are all applications that are routinely addressed by the application of molecular biology methods.

For example, Molecular biology is already showing a great impact in the diagnosis and treatment for cancer. This new technology has identified specific DNA sequences linked to genetic diseases and made carrier detection and prenatal diagnosis routine. Molecular probes are also used widely for rapid and specific identification of infectious agents and in various aspects of forensic medicine.

Molecular diagnoses are making use of exciting new techniques, such as nanotechnology. Nanoscale devices, quantum dots, and carbon nanotubes, are all cutting edge and promising nanotools for the effective measurement of malignancy. All these techniques offer great promise for revolutionising the diagnosis of cancer.

And, just as quantum technologies develop as a whole, so will Quantum Medicine. We will be able to analyse a person's DNA structure to the smallest of molecules, and, thanks to powerful quantum computers, we will be able run models to maximise overall health.

However, as we saw in the section on epigenetics, DNA itself is not set in stone and is prone to change as a result of environmental factors. Therefore, the power of genetic material and what we do with it will still lie within ourselves. Having a deeper understanding of the boundaries of our unique genetic structure, with its predetermined strengths and weaknesses, shouldn't mean that we accept a label and lie back doing nothing about it.

Quite the opposite, it will be the ultimate form of constructive feedback: if you know, from the moment you are born, that you will be prone to diabetes, you will have a lifetime of personal choices ahead of you to make sure that doesn't happen.

By personalising medicine to a quantum level, we will discover new depths of our uniqueness, even at a deeper level than genetics allows. And once we start to use Quantum Psychology to unveil the potential within ourselves, we will also grasp our power and responsibility to overcome almost any genetic handicap or diseases that we might experience in life. This, combined with the diagnostic and treatment techniques that will arise, will allow us to live much longer lives, perhaps hundreds of years, thanks to the implications of our own connection with the Quantum Realm and the vision of Quantum Medicine.

CHAPTER 14: THE CORE OF QUANTUM PSYCHOLOGY

We have covered how Quantum Psychology can act as the bridge uniting all scales of physics and bringing sense and meanings to our existence. Furthermore, following the Quantum Self, we find our consciousness as the centre of everything, including the Universe itself. But what lies at the centre of that centre, providing meaning, purpose, and direction to all that immeasurable energy contained within each one of us?

In this chapter, we will explore how our subjective emotions, motivations, subjective happiness and karma (understood from the Quantum Psychology perspective) play a key role in connecting us with to our Quantum Self. Throughout the definitions, and some of the scientific research evidence, we have seen hints of how the way we develop those cognitive traits has an impact on almost every aspect of our life.

Misalignment of any of these factors could cause an imbalance that sets toxic patterns in motion, distorting how reality unfolds for us. Because, before our biological and social cognition can label and give meaning to those emotions, motivations, subjective happiness or karma, they are made of the raw and uncontrollable sensations that come from our connections with others and the Quantum Realm, hinting to us that what we are truly transcends this life.

14.1. How Do We Learn & Experience Emotions?

A true, visceral, and deeply felt emotion is the essence of any important decision we make in life. However, and even if we experience hundreds of emotions on a daily basis, accurately defining them has been a challenge for researchers and philosophers for centuries. Furthermore, when it comes to figuring out how we learn to express and interpret all those emotions, cultural, and inter or intra-personal differences seem to play a decisive role.

Emotion, by its most general definition, is a neural impulse that moves an organism to action, prompting automatic reactive behaviour, which has been adapted as a survival mechanism through evolution to meet a survival need.

Emotions seem to rule our daily lives. We make decisions based on whether we are happy, angry, sad, bored, or frustrated. We choose activities and hobbies based on the emotions they incite. According to the book "*Discovering Psychology*" by Don Hockenbury and Sandra E. Hockenbury, an emotion is a complex psychological state that involves three distinct components: a subjective experience, a physiological response, and a behavioural or expressive response.

Emotions are generally classified as primary or secondary. The most fundamental emotions, known as the primary or basic emotions, are those of *anger, disgust, fear, happiness, sadness, and surprise*. Basic emotions have a long history in human evolution. They have developed in large part to help us make rapid judgments about stimuli, and to quickly guide appropriate behaviour.

A large body of research has shown that the basic emotions are determined in large part by one of the oldest parts of our brain, the limbic system, including the amygdala, the hypothalamus, and the thalamus. Because they are primarily evolutionarily determined, the basic emotions are experienced and displayed in much the same way across cultures, and people are able to accurately judge the facial expressions of people from different cultures.

On the other hand, it has also been found that secondary emotions are more culturally determined and are often activated in very particular situations. Although they are largely cognitive, our experiences of the secondary emotions are determined in part by arousal and in part by their valence – that is, whether they are pleasant or unpleasant feelings. Secondary emotions in the brain follow a slow pathway through the frontal lobes in the cortex, with the thalamus acting as the major gatekeeper.

From a psychological point of view, the component of emotions that scientists call subjective feelings refer to the way each individual person experiences feelings, this component is the most difficult to describe or measure. Subjective feelings cannot be observed; instead, the person experiencing the emotion must describe it to others, and each person's description and interpretation of a feeling may be slightly different. For example, two people falling in love will not experience or describe their feeling in exactly the same way.

From a social perspective, research data from around the world showed little difference in people's day-to-day emotional experiences. However, there were reliable differences in ideal affects. When asked about how they would ideally like to feel, Europeans and Americans typically preferred excitement and elation more than did Chinese, who preferred calm and relaxation more. This difference in ideal affect shows up in children's books, magazine ads, and the official portraits of politicians and business leaders. Therefore, this could indicate that the way we learn to experience emotions can be influenced in early stages of development.

From a pedagogical angle, emotional development is a complex task that begins in infancy and continues into adulthood. The first emotions that can be recognised in babies include joy, anger, sadness and fear. Later, as children begin to develop a sense of self, more complex emotions like shyness, surprise, elation, embarrassment, shame, guilt, pride and empathy emerge.

As children develop, the things that provoke their emotional responses change, as do the strategies they use to manage them.

The attachment relationship with caregivers is the initial context in which a child's emotional life unfolds. It is commonly accepted that if the caregivers typically meet the infant's needs, the infant comes to internalise the notion that the world is a safe place and that others are trustworthy and responsive. The caregiver-child relationship establishes the foundation for the development of emotional skills and sets the stage for future social relationships.

In contrast, a child who experiences the world as unpredictable, unresponsive and/or hostile must expend a tremendous amount of energy self-managing emotional arousal. Insecure attachment is associated with emotional and social incompetence. For example, a child who experiences maltreatment may develop primary emotional responses such as anxiety or fear.

The ability to develop emotional attachments and healthy connections is also shaped by what is known as Emotional Intelligence, popularised by Daniel Goleman Emotional Intelligence is the ability to recognise your emotions, understand what they're telling you, and realise how your emotions affect people around you. It also involves your perception of others: when you understand how they feel, this allows you to manage relationships more effectively.

There is no doubt that early experiences have a profound influence on the developing brain and behaviour, with early environments shaping neuro-affective trajectories and long-term adult phenotypes of emotional behaviour. From a wider perspective of how we learn different cognitive skills (such as language, memory or attention), research shows that early childhood is marked by critical periods – times when the brain is intensely adaptable to new sights, sounds, tastes, and touches, making a person highly susceptible to learning a particular skill.

During this window, we assimilate and internalise the way we will perceive and express emotions for the rest of our life. Therefore, if during this critical period a person has been emotionally neglected, he/she will struggle to experience and develop a healthy and balanced emotional experience throughout life.

For example, say that a person grows up in a family with parents that hate each other and were only able to communicate their feelings through hostility. It is likely that the child will interpret love as some sort of intense, toxic, and mean emotion to be expressed with everything but caring, internalising this interpretation as she/he grows up. However, recent studies suggest it may be possible to extend critical periods. Just as when we lose sight, the rest of our senses are enhanced, our cognitive system has the resources to be trained and improved throughout life, and all you need is the right tools, mind-set and motivation.

From the perspective of Quantum Psychology, the way we create and experience an emotion is hugely impacted by our Quantum Self, and vice versa. As mentioned in the section on the afterlife, the raw inner sensations we experience when connecting with others and our environment is what is left of us when we pass. While we are alive, these honest sensations are the ultimate connection between our Quantum Self and the physical world we inhabit. Emotions are what we experience once our biological and social self-labels are turned off, giving context to those raw reactions and connections that emanate from the core of our soul.

Have you ever wondered why most of our emotions don't comply with reason or logic, running wild and leading us to act and make decisions that sometimes seem to make no sense? This is because their primal ingredient is made from the core of our consciousness, our Quantum Self, where the rules and conclusions made are not tied to the narrow limitations of our time and space related biology. In order to reach a conclusion at an emotional level, factors that escape our conscious awareness have been taken into consideration, invoking our deeply entangled and connected instincts.

Because of this, our emotions will always hold a powerful and indivisible force over us. They will always be behind any big decision we will make in life; being the sustenance to what motivates us; giving a sense of meaning and purpose to our most important tasks and achievements. And all because they are the essence that connects our biological self with our Quantum Self, lying beneath the limitations of life and reality as we know it.

And, above all the emotions we experience, inter-biological love is the strongest, most elemental and quantum connected emotion that there is. Everyone experiences love in different ways: the way you understand romantic or fraternal love applies only to you – and the different self-defined experiences and expectation of love is why many relationships cannot last. Furthermore, we do not love two people exactly the same way, and even the way we love someone might change and evolve over time – just as the connections we establish are unique and variable over time.

However, if we experience emotions in dysfunctional ways (perhaps because of how we assimilated them during our critical period), we will set ourselves up to establish those kinds of toxic connections, feeding our own expectations, and forming a self-reinforcing vicious circle. And, since the psychological principle of "wanting to be right" is so strong, breaking the negative pattern can be extremely hard.

It is, therefore, of the greatest importance to learn how to appropriately experience and interpret love. Moreover, we often confuse love with an attraction to the material things that we like. For example, saying "*I love Lego*", despite my strong and binding emotion towards that hobby, shouldn't be mistaken with the act of loving, which necessarily involves a quantum and energetic connection of some sort with another biological being. Love is the defining emotion that connects us to the rest of the Universe, and the most direct line between ourselves and everything and everyone else at a biological or quantum level. Love is at the centre of our consciousness and Quantum Self, which sits at the centre of the Universe and reality.

It is true that there are many different ways of loving someone: romantically, platonically, familiarly... You can even experience love for a living being from another species. In the name of love, you will find every single extreme of your nature, as it never comes in a temperate temperature. If you love someone in a healthy way, that love will only enhance yourself and everyone that is touched by that love; on the other hand, if you assimilate love as part of suffering, anyone that you love will become part of that suffering and will weigh you down at the same time.

Love is subjective and intense; it cannot be tamed by reason or logic. By its raw, deep, and innate nature it represents the most direct connection we have with the Quantum Realm, and the strongest line to shape and determine the outcomes of our world. When you are motivated by love, you are in direct contact with all the quantum possibilities of the reality being unfolded to you. As a result, loving in a healthy manner might be one of the most difficult things to achieve in life, as its purity can so easily be stained by corrupted emotions.

The purest and strongest endeavours will be made in the name of love. Love is the key to fully understanding our real power and influence on the way our world is unveiled to us, when all the quantum possibilities collapse into the final materialisation. Do not make the mistake of taking love for granted; be ready to enhance your self-awareness and challenge every aspect of the way you have learned that love should be.

Then, once you feel it, follow the path love marks you to follow, and do not let anything or anyone take your determination and conviction away from it, because only by following that tortuous and senseless trail will you encounter the highest meaning of life.

14.2. The Importance of Motivation

One of the biggest challenges in achieving any goal is finding the motivation to pursue it with perseverance. If you can stick to fighting for a goal long enough, you'll almost always get there, eventually. It just takes patience, resilience, determination, conviction and, above all, motivation. Motivation is what drives you towards a goal, what keeps you going when things get tough, the reason you get up early to exercise or work late to finish a project.

There are all kinds of motivations, of course, from positive to negative. Having a boss threaten to fire you is motivation – you will likely work harder to complete a project with that kind of pressure. But usually positive motivation works best – if it's something you really want to do, you will do a much better job than if the motivation is avoiding something you don't want (such as being fired). So, motivation, in its best form, is a way for you to want to do something.

To trace the source of motivation, let's begin in the brain where neurotransmitters spark chemical messages to keep us alert and on task. One neurotransmitter that plays a role in motivation is dopamine. Essentially, your brain recognises that something important is about to happen, so dopamine kicks in, sparking your motivation.

From a psychological perspective, most motivational theories differentiate between intrinsic and extrinsic factors: the former are concerned with an individual's interest, enjoyment, and willingness to partake in an activity. People with higher self-confidence and belief that their own abilities will lead to success are more likely to have high levels of intrinsic motivation. Extrinsic motivations focus on the outcome of the activity i.e. individuals are driven by the outcome rather than the activity itself.

From a functional point of view, we can distinguish between content and process theories of motivation. Content theories focus on WHAT, while process theories focus on HOW human behaviour is motivated. Content theories are the earliest theories of motivation and are also called needs theories: they try to identify what our needs are and relate motivation to the fulfilling of these needs. The main content theories are: Maslow's hierarchy of needs, Alderfer's Existence, Relatedness, Growth (ERG) theory, McClelland's achievement motivation and Herzberg's two-factor theory.

Process theories are concerned with "how" motivation occurs, and what kind of process can influence our motivation. The main process theories are: Skinner's reinforcement theory, Victor Vroom's expectancy theory, Adam's equity theory and Locke's goal setting theory.

No single motivation theory explains all aspects of people's motivation or lack of motivation. Each theoretical explanation can serve as the basis for the development of techniques for motivating. However, there is one particular theory that deserves closer attention: Maslow's Hierarchy of Needs Theory.

Maslow's theory is based on the human needs; drawing chiefly on his clinical experience, he classified all human needs into a hierarchical manner from the lower to the higher order. In essence, he believed that once a given level of need is satisfied, it no longer serves to motivate a person. Then, the next higher level of need has to be activated in order to motivate. Maslow identified five levels in his need hierarchy:

- Physiological needs: such as hunger, thirst and sleep.

- Safety needs: such as security, protection from danger and freedom from pain.

- Social needs: referred to as love needs such as friendship, giving and receiving love, engaging in social activities and group membership.

- Esteem needs: these include both self-respect and the esteem of others; for example, the desire for self-confidence, achievement, recognition and appreciation.

- Self-actualisation: This is about the desire to develop and realise your full potential. To become everything you can be.

Despite the wide acceptance of this theory, many have criticised it on different grounds. For instance, researchers have proved that needs have no hierarchical structure, though every individual has some ordering the satisfaction of his/her needs. Another problem is that there is a lack of a direct cause-and-effect relationship between need and behaviour. One particular need may cause different types of behaviours in different people. On the other hand, a particular individual behaviour may be due to the result of different needs. Thus, need hierarchy is not as simple as it appears to be. Finally, another problem with Maslow's theory of motivation is the implementation of some of his concepts, which make it difficult for researchers to test his theory. For instance, how does one measure self-actualisation?

In an ideal world, we would never worry about something in the upper levels of needs until everything below is satisfied, but that's just not how it tends to happen. Our own personal motivations can be biased or driven by factors that go way beyond our logical needs.

Emotions, achievement of bigger picture goals, or our psychological health, have a deterministic impact on where and how our motivation develops overtime, and at the same time, our level of motivation has a direct impact on everything we do, either consciously or subconsciously.

As a result, the ebbs and flows of our motivation will act as a trans-linking force to affect other *links* throughout the network. If your general motivation were affected, most likely your attention would also shift. This could start a chain reaction of a new pattern of behaviour. And, as this path is reinforced overtime, its effects will also grow exponentially.

Being able to understand, control, and develop your motivation will enhance your chances of pursuing whatever goal you have in mind. However, there are no set rules that magically work on everyone to increase motivation. Quite the opposite, this is a process of self-introspection and trial-and-error where you must learn what works best for you under a specific circumstance and at a given time.

But, make no mistake; motivation is the impulse required to set the rest of your machinery in motion. Having a clear and healthy motivation will be a huge advantage in achieving anything you want in life. In terms of motivation, the worst and most dangerous phenomena you can experience will be the lack of it. Without motivation, we are barely robots, without a purpose; without motivation, the strong and resilient seed of depression can be planted in the core of your soul. And, if left to grow, it will conquer, spreading its weeds in every aspect of your life, ultimately taking away your will to thrive and grow.

14.3. The Subjectivity of Happiness

We have previously covered what subjective well-being means and how it affects and influences our self-development. Often subjective well-being is confused with happiness, although there are some key differences between the two concepts. Most researchers use happiness to mean nothing more than a state of mind, like being satisfied with your life or having a positive emotional condition. By contrast, researchers normally use well-being to denote a kind of value. This value concerns what benefits or harms you or makes you better or worse off. To ask what well-being is, then, is to ask what is ultimately good for people, with a higher social consensus than the subjectivity of happiness offers.

Research suggests that happiness is a combination of how satisfied you are with your life (for example, finding meaning in your work) and how good you feel on a day-to-day basis. The good news is, with consistent effort, this can be offset. Think of it like you think about weight: if you eat how you want to and are as active as you want to be, your body will settle at a certain weight. But if you eat less than you'd like or exercise more, your weight will adjust accordingly. If that new diet or exercise regimen becomes part of your everyday life, then you'll stay at this new weight. If you go back to eating and exercising the way you used to, your weight will return to where it started. So it goes, too, with happiness.

In other words, you have the ability to influence how you feel – and with consistent practice, you can form lifelong habits for a more satisfying and fulfilling life. A "happy person" experiences the spectrum of emotions just like anybody else, but the frequency by which they experience the negative ones may differ. It could be that "happy people" don't experience as much negative emotion because they process it differently or they may find meaning in a way others have not. Nobody is immune to life's stressors, but the question is whether you see those stressors as moments of opposition or moments of opportunity.

From a philosophical perspective, there are three theories of happiness. First, there is *hedonism*. In all its variants, it holds that happiness is a matter of raw subjective feeling. A happy life maximises feelings of pleasure and minimises pain. A happy person smiles a lot, is ebullient, bright eyed and bushy tailed; pleasures are intense and many, pains are few and far between.

Secondly, *desire* theories hold that happiness is a matter of getting what you want, with the content of the want left up to the person who does the wanting. Desire theories subsumes hedonism when what we want is lots of pleasure and little pain. Like hedonism, desire theory can explain why an ice-cream cone is preferable to a poke in the eye. However, hedonism and desire theory often part company. Hedonism holds that the preponderance of pleasure over pain is the recipe for happiness even if this is not what one desires most. Desire theory holds that that fulfilment of a desire contributes to one's happiness regardless of the amount of pleasure (or displeasure).

Lastly, *objective list* theories lodges happiness outside of feeling and onto a list of "truly valuable" things in the real world. It holds that happiness consists of a human life that achieves certain things from a list of worthwhile pursuits: career accomplishments, friendship, freedom from disease and pain, material comforts, civic spirit, beauty, education, love, knowledge, and good conscience. However, given the individual approaches and coping strategies when facing identical situations, setting an objective bar to define happiness seems implausible. Happiness comes from choosing to be happy with whatever you do, strengthening your closest relationships and taking care of yourself physically, financially, and emotionally.

Whichever theory you think fits best with your own understanding and experience of happiness, what seems clear is that happier people tend to live longer, healthier lives, make more money and do better at work. It's a chicken and egg problem, though. Does happiness bring those kinds of things, or do those kinds of things lead us to be happier?

Above all the previous considerations, happiness is a subjective point of view, or a personal opinion. What makes you satisfied and happy might be insufficient to others, or vice versa. Furthermore, what makes you happy now, might not make you happy in the future.

The concept of subjective happiness is closely tied to our emotions and motivations, and they all tend to work in parallel: if you experience more positive emotions in a healthy way, it is likely that you will also feel more motivated towards achieving your goals, and that you will subjectively be happier. And, overall, your existence will feel good and meaningful.

But why is it that way? Our Quantum Self acts as the director of that orchestra, where time and space can be partly shaped and determined depending on our emotions, motivations, and level of happiness. If we are balanced in these, we will project an attuned energetic message onto the world, which will also be perceived by those around us. Then, you will set in motion a positive and adaptive self-reinforced cycle, or karma.

As a final reflection, if you consciously train yourself to always see the glass of your happiness as half full, then you are already interpreting whatever comes back from the world from a positive perspective, since we always want to be right. So, since how to interpret a given situation is totally and subjectively up to you, what is stopping you from being on the happy side?

14.4. Did You Say Karma?

As Western culture has become more aware of the concept of karma, its meaning and implications have quite regularly been misinterpreted. And, although I will present and explain the definition and implications of karma from the traditional perspective of Eastern philosophy, I will also link it with the Quantum Realm.

Karma is a central concept in Eastern religions such as Hinduism, Buddhism, Sikhism and Jainism. The word "karma" has its roots in the Sanskrit word "karman," which means "act". In general, it is believed that actions affect the quality of life and the quality of future lives. Good deeds create good karma and evil deeds create negative karma. Traditionally, karma's effect can manifest immediately, later in life or after multiple lifetimes. Some religions view karma as the law that governs reincarnation. Others believe that karma is actual particulate matter, something that gets stuck to the soul and must be removed through acts of piety.

In the West, the relatively modern idea of karma is not so much a spiritual reality as type of luck influenced by deeds. It is an appealing attempt to influence fortune – something seemingly beyond our control – with definite action. As if good behaviour merited a divine reward and bad behaviour warranted punishment. In a rational age, karma is a popular and fairly legitimate form of superstition. However, this western perception seems suspiciously linked with the traditional Christian morals, or a tool through which to externally dictate how we should behave, leaving out of the equation our individual power.

People dismissively say: "it's my karma", suggesting that their destiny or fate is merely the luck of the draw or bad fortune. Applying the concept in this way suggests a lack of power or personal responsibility for being both the cause and the effect of what occurs in one's life. Using the phrase "it's my karma" suggests victimhood, and karma is anything but victimhood. It's also talked about as if this currency stays with you until things are "evened out".

Karma doesn't literally mean that if you do something good then good things will inevitably come back to you, like some invisible tracking system that links bad people to punishment and good people to rewards. It does mean, however, that by seeking to do the right thing in any given situation you, as well as those around, will become conditioned for peace and happiness in a very real and concrete way. Likewise, through negative actions you condition yourself as well as those around you for suffering now and in the future. It is misguided to believe we need anything outside of ourselves in order to be happy. It's because of this false view that we desire to transform karma into a sort of cash machine based on ethical and spiritual behaviour.

Karma means action. Newtonian physics shows that for every action, there must be an equal and opposite reaction. Karma is energy, which in itself is neither good nor bad; these are just the labels people choose to attach to it. The energy created by an action has to be returned: as yea sow, so shall yea reap. It cannot be avoided.

From a Quantum Psychology perspective, the concept of karma should be separated from mythology or superstition, and integrated with our sensory, cognitive, and Quantum Self. Karma can be understood as somewhat of an aggregate on how we transmit to the world the energetic message shaped by our emotions, motivations and happiness. And, just like them, karma is subjective in nature.

You can do something over and over again, evaluating it as something positive and meaningful. Therefore, your emotions, motivations and general happiness will transmit your positivity and balance into the Universe. As a result, people and the energy around you will pick up that message and respond to it in an equivalent way.

This continuous interaction between our Quantum Self and the rest of the world sets a blueprint that shapes what we get back from our environment. The bottom line is, if you feel well about yourself when evaluating whether your actions are rightful, then you will create good karma for yourself and you will be likely to experience positivity in return.

On the contrary, if you feel guilt or shame regarding actions or aspects of your life, you are creating bad karma for yourself. Then, your Quantum Self will look for the equivalent negative and toxic energy around you. Basically, you will be telling the scope of quantum possibilities that you would prefer those that equal your own negativity.

Despite being influenced by cultural and social factors, we ultimately control karma. For example, in some societies certain behaviour can be perceived as undesirable, while in others the same action will be tolerated or even encouraged. People born and raised in the suppressive environment and behaving accordingly will be more likely to feel guilt, compared to those that grow up in a tolerant society.

Even if the accumulation of negative sensations might lead to the creation of negative karma, you still have the ultimate power to shape your karma and influence the outcome of what happens to you. Therefore, all it takes to create good karma is to believe that what you do and how you experience life is positive and meaningful.

Do you want good things to happen to you and to experience more positive emotions, happiness and motivation? All you need is to decide to take it, because no one will give it to you. There is no magic formula to grab it and evaluate your life and others from a positive point of view. However, if you keep finding yourself unable to do so, ask yourself: what's stopping me from deciding to take charge of my perception and selecting what I want my life to turn into?

CHAPTER 15: DESTINY VS. FREE WILL

Let's imagine the following experiment: an electronic device is designed to flip a coin after a person presses a button to eject it. In order to control all the atmospheric variables, the device is encapsulated in a glass wide enough to ensure the flipped coin will never impact it. Furthermore, the temperature, humidity and atmospheric pressure in the room are kept stable, and the strength applied by the machine when throwing the coin is identical every time. The coins to be flipped are made by the same machine, using the same materials, and making sure their shape and weight are absolutely indistinguishable. Each coin is also placed in exactly the same position in the device before being flipped.

Therefore, we have a device that is totally isolated from any external influence, which will apply the same force over and over to flip identical coins once the researcher presses a button to activate the mechanism. Will the coin land exactly the same way every time, considering all physical variables are controlled, or will we still find the statistically expected randomness in the results?

This is only a conceptual experimental paradigm, never performed or tested. However, your preconception of what would happen can reveal your beliefs about whether our fate is determined by destiny or free will. Furthermore, the results and possible variations of the experiment (like making a double blind experiment where the person pressing the button wouldn't know what it is for at all, or asking that person to consciously think about getting more heads than tails, for instance) could cast some light in the matter.

Are we puppets of life, controlled by a set destiny crafted by external divine forces, or is each moment a clean slate ruled by complete unpredictability of what happens next, fuelled by our free will?

15.1. Destiny

"A consistent man believes in destiny, a capricious man in chance." So replied Benjamin Disraeli, when asked which of the above two life-directing factors had played a major role in determining his destiny as a politician and statesman.

The dichotomy of destiny versus free will has been a widely debated topic for centuries. Earlier traditions tended to believe that Gods preordain the inescapable destiny of each individual life. After the influence of philosophers such as Democritus and Aristotle, a more rational view prevailed, based on the theory of Determinism, which stipulating that a human being, like all forms of being in the Universe, is just one phenomenological manifestation of existence in a continuous series of on-going cosmic creations taking place on this planet, all the result of sheer causal necessity in an evolving Universe.

Destiny is defined as: "a predetermined course of events considered as something beyond human power or control". From this perspective, all our physiological and psychological complexity is just a part of a (perhaps unique) bio-living entity occupying the earth. As such, the course of your life will basically be determined by the positive or negative factors built-in to your genetic inheritance.

Destiny means that which you cannot avoid; from which there is no escape. Religion has often embraced a belief in set destiny. If you believe in a God, then you likely believe that God is responsible for the creation of the universe and all of the happenings within it. Everything that happens in every person's life is God's will. But what about free will?

15.2. Free Will

Free Will is commonly understood as those impulses of thought and feeling that allow one to make choices, and decisions, directly affecting and shaping the course of our life. More formally, free will is defined as: "The ability or discretion to choose. The power of making choices that are neither determined by natural causality nor predestined by fate or divine will".

Psychologically, the force we call the Will, can be understood as the operational side of the force we think of as spirit: that they are partners in a mental process operating beyond the normal sensory and rational workings of consciousness.

However, what we call free will might not be free at all; it could be dependent, conditioned, fickle and not our own at all. From this perspective, it could be implied that your "will" is dependent on your gender, nationality, age, religion, or even on your mood. And, when your will depends on so many things, can it really be considered free?

In fact, there is the taunting scientific theory claiming that we do not hold any power at all when it comes to making any given decision; stating that free will is nothing more than an illusion. This scientific trend has denied the existence of free will for over two decades, arguing that human behaviour is governed by the brain, which is itself controlled by each person's genetic blueprint, built upon by her or his life experiences.

In recent years, neuroscience has found interesting evidence to support this conclusion. In one experiment, subjects were asked to make a flick of their wrist at a time of their own choosing, and to note the position of the second hand of a clock at the moment of choosing. However, simultaneous recordings of the subjects' brain activity showed that preparations for movement were occurring about half a second before the conscious decision to move. Subsequent experiments have confirmed these findings. Scientists concluded that our decisions are being driven by unconscious brain activity, not by conscious choice. But when the decision reaches conscious awareness, we experience having made a choice.

From this perspective, the apparent freedom of choice lies in our not knowing what the outcome will be. Take, for example, the common process of choosing what to eat in a restaurant. I first eliminate dishes I don't like, or ones I ate recently, narrowing down to a few that attract me. I then decide on one of these according to various other factors – nutritional value, tastes, what I feel my body needs, etc. It feels like I am making a free choice, but the decision I come to, is predetermined by current circumstances and past experience. However, because I do not know the outcome of the decision-making process until it appears in my mind, I feel that I have made a free choice.

Yet, the other side of the conundrum persists. The experience of making choices of our own volition is very real. And we live our lives on the assumption that we are making decisions of our own free will and directing our own future. It is virtually impossible not to. Implicit in the notion of choice is the existence of a "chooser" – an independent self that is an active agent in the process. This, too, fits with our experience. There seems to be an "I" that perceives the world, making assessments and decisions, and making its own choices. This "I" feels it has chosen the dish from the menu. The experience of an individual self is so intrinsic to our lives that we seldom doubt its veracity. But does it really exist in its own right? Two lines of research suggest not.

Neuroscientists find no evidence of an individual self located somewhere in the brain. Instead they propose that what we call "I" is but a mental construct derived from bodily experience. We draw a distinction between "me" and "not me" and create a sense of self for the "me" part. From a biological point of view, this distinction is most valuable. Taking care of the needs of this self, is taking care of our physical needs. We seek whatever promotes our well-being and avoid anything that threatens it.

The second, very different, line of research involves the exploration of subjective experience. People who have delved into the nature of the actual experience of self have discovered that the closer they examine this sense of "I", the more it seems to dissolve. Time and again they find there are no independent self. There are thoughts of "I", but no "I" that is thinking them.

Nevertheless – and this is critical for resolving the paradox – in our everyday state of consciousness, the sense of self is very real. It is who we are. Although this "I" may be part of the brain's model of reality, it is nevertheless intimately involved in the making of decisions, weighing up the pros and cons, coming to conclusions, choosing what to do and when to do it. So, in the state where the self is real, we do experience ourselves making choices. And those choices are experienced as being of our own volition. Here, free will is real.

15.3. Actually: Free Will AND Destiny

The riddle of destiny versus free will has traditionally been presented as a mutually excluding one, however, there are perspectives that present it as more of a continuum, a spectrum with the reality lying somewhere in the middle. From these perspectives a combination of destiny and free will rule our lives.

Although we cannot know for certain whether destiny, free will, or both, govern our lives, we are capable of feeling what guides us. Sometimes, the feeling of what guides us is so strong, that it takes control of our lives. We may feel a God, or any other superior entity is guiding us; we may feel fate guiding us; we may feel only free will guiding us; and so on.

Free will and determinism are no longer paradoxical in the sense of being mutually exclusive. Both are correct, depending upon the consciousness from which they are considered. The paradox only appears when we consider both sides from the same state of consciousness, i.e. the everyday waking state. As when Hamlet pondered the question of *"To be or not to be?"* The character in the play is making a choice. And if we have not seen the play before, we may wonder which way he will choose. This is the thrill of the play, to be engaged in it, moved by it, absorbed in its reality with all its twists and turns.

However, we also know that William Shakespeare determined how the play unfolds long ago. So, we have two complementary ways of viewing the play. At times we may choose to live fully in the drama. Other times we may step back to admire his creative genius. In life, we can be engaged in the drama, experiencing free will, making choices that affect our futures. Or we can step back and be a witness to this amazing play of life unfolding before us. Both are true within their respective frameworks.

Each of us choose our own endings and destinies through the words, thoughts and actions we choose every day. Through our character and who we are as people. There is a cause to every effect and there is a reaction to every action. We have the power to change at any time we choose, for better or worse. All of our choices have consequences. And, as Quantum Psychology insists, the real power lies within us.

15.3. The Will of the Quantum Self

Remember that Quantum Mechanics is based on a world of possibilities, and not certainties. And it is only when forced to make a choice that subatomic particles adjust to our own time and space limitations. Similarly, when we are forced to make (sub) conscious decisions, it is only then that our mind will weight all the possible factors and sources of information available to make that choice. But, as we make decisions almost continuously, we need some cognitive shortcuts (like cognitive biases, for example) in order to keep up with our immediate environmental threats and not exhaust our mental energy.

As a result, we make those bigger or smaller decisions depending on how crucial, subjectively important, and interdependent (like genetic structure, previous experiences, expectations, attention, motivation...) we experience them to be.. Quantum Psychology adds another factor weighing on those decisions. This is the part where our free will becomes real. All the possibilities to choose from are in front of us, and we come up with conclusions after combining all the available information, choosing one path and not other (whether it is the right one or not).

But, as we have just seen, this concept has been challenged by science, arguing that our brain is tricking us into believing so. However, this perspective shows at least four important limitations. Firstly, our brain is still part of ourselves; therefore, arguing that our brain making the first step into the decision-making process means that everything is determined in life is deceiving, as it is not an external force manipulating us to go one way or another, but our own nervous system.

Secondly, the brain is constantly active. Therefore, it seems very bold to claim that we can completely isolate the course of action of a decision made from a neurological point of view, without assuming that this process has been triggered by previous or parallel brain activity; in other words, you cannot read a random word from a book and presume that you know what the book is about, you would need to read a bigger portion of the text to start understanding the story.

Thirdly, the types of decisions studied in the research are rather simple tasks, involving very few cognitive resources. As we dive into more complex decision-making, the number of factors and length of the process will also increase exponentially. Furthermore, you will need to account for inter-individual and intra-individual differences, where our most recent brain activity will not be the only source when making a vital life changing decision about something.

Lastly, the Quantum Self has a role to play. If a part of our (sub) consciousness interacts with the Quantum Realm and drives back some of the possible outcomes of a decision, then such information drawn back to our mind will hold an important influence into the final decision. The weight of our Quantum Self in making a given decision will likely also increase, as we perceive it as important, challenging, or complex.

In those cases, we will be very motivated to make the right call by analysing (sometimes even too much) all the information available to us. And, since the Quantum Realm doesn't understand the limitations time and space, sometimes that information will come from one of the possible outcomes our decisions can lead to. Therefore, sometimes you will feel the urge to make an important decision, even if you are not totally aware of why – a sort of hint from your Quantum Self. Then, once that decision is made and you discover the consequences, you will suddenly fully understand why you were "meant" to make that decision.

Therefore, once we wield our free will; we set the bases for a sort of "interactive destiny" or fate. This means that opting for one thing instead of other options will set the consequences to come, even if we are not able to anticipate the final outcome.

As an example, say you are trying to decide what to eat today: you will consider all available options, weighting all the information you have at hand, and then make your preferred choice of restaurant. This is the part belonging to your free will, and your fate will be pre-determined based on that. Your obvious anticipation is that the consequence is that you will end up eating in the restaurant you chose.

However, say that on your way to that restaurant, you jump into an old friend you haven't seen in a while and engage in conversation. As you both are happy to see each other, and since your friend has no time to go to the restaurant you previously chose, you both end up going to a nearby place to eat and catch up. During that meeting, the conversation turns out to be highly productive and you actually start to talk about a venture business opportunity interesting for the both of you. That business idea, further down the line, turns out to be one that changes your life completely. And it all started by freely making a rather small decision like picking up a restaurant. Yet, for the rest of your life, you will somewhat feel that you were supposed to make that small choice, so that you could meet your friend and change your life.

It might sound like an extreme example, however similar situations will happen to you a handful of times during your lifespan. For those choices, if we are aware and sensitive enough to listen to it, it will be the Quantum Self weighing in heavily and pushing us to make an apparently unimportant decision in one direction and not another,

Another point to take into consideration is our own processing mechanism, which can be more, or less, adaptive. Sometimes you might be tied to toxic patterns of behaviour that will cloud your decision-making process and those Quantum signs portraying beneficial outcomes. Once again, your mind always wants to be right. Remember one thing: no one will ever punish you in your life as much as you will punish your self. Hence the importance of following your inner instinct, even when it doesn't make sense to you yet, further down the line, it will.

Finally, as we take one decision, we will be confronted with many more decisions to make, which eventually affect and change the "predetermined" outcome drawn by the initial decision, taking you down another path. This means that the decision-making journey is a very interactive and complex one, filled with constant distractions and alternatives that continuously shape your destination. Both free will and destiny are constantly re-shaped from the reality of possibilities of the Quantum Realm.

Coming back to the experimental coin-flipping device from the beginning, what do you think now? Will the coin always draw the same parabola in the air, falling in exactly the same position, or will it be an unplanned result, as if your hand flipped it? Could our consciousness have any degree of influence in this outcome, as we can on randomly generated numbers or circles in a computer?

Our free will is the best way to set our fate and write in stone the determinism of the world we create. Deciding based on your Quantum Self is the richest way to control your predetermined destiny.

CHAPTER 16: SO, WHAT'S IN QUANTUM PSYCHOLOGY FOR ME?

If you made it this far through the book, most likely some of the contents and ideas shared have somehow made an impact on you – whether positive or negative. To be honest, the direction of that impression doesn't really matter. Because all that is important is generating that raw sensation within the core of your being, emanating from your Quantum Self. Then, from there, the valance that our biological and social self assigns to it is secondary.

Besides, as I stated at the beginning, this is not a self-help book at all. This is not the type of reading where I pretend to present any kind of indisputable truth. In fact, I hope you had a sceptical and critical mind all along. The way I have presented the reality of our objective Universe and us as beings is certainly from a subjective point of view. This is the terminology and perspective that I chose to understand who we are, where we come from, and what we should expect going forward.

The ultimate goal of this manuscript in particular, and of Quantum Psychology in general, is not to bring definite answers straight away, but to raise your curiosity, for you to ask your own questions, so that we may move closer to definite answers, and especially those that are meaningful on a personal level.

I believe that, at the most intrinsic and elemental level, everything that we are is shared by every living creature in the entire Universe. That's the beauty of it: it is close to impossible to accurately describe, with precise detail, every single implication and sensation originating from our Quantum Self. However, the moments when we experience it are so universal that everyone can relate to them and bring to their memory exact situations where they felt in touch with something bigger than the self and biological life.

However, we cannot forget or ignore that we are living organisms, tied to the necessary limitations of perception and awareness, skewed by our imperative and timelessly reinforced instinct of immediate survival. Limitations of time are necessary for our minds to discern between what belongs to the past, present, or future; limitations of space are necessary as our bodies encapsulate and determine the physical proximity of our environment; and, of course, our cognitive limitations, narrowing our vision and understanding of the rules that qualify a being as 'alive', are necessary to make sense of the myriad of sensations and information constantly available to us.

Nevertheless, it is in those inherited limitations that we can find our biggest strengths, which carry us towards a higher version of ourselves as a species. Because it is thanks to the way our brains and bodies work that we can accomplish pretty much anything we set our minds to. Our success is thanks to our imagination, to our ability to experience and evaluate feelings, to our memories that consciously anchor us to those moments of true connection. It is because we live in a biologically limited plane of existence, that we can access our unique individuality and ultimate freedom: the power to decide, every instant of counted and perishable time, what we do with that untameable source of energy that we all belong to.

Everything created and existing in this Universe starts from us, and not the other way around. We, as living entities holding part of that source and current of quantum energy, are the reason for creation to exist. Without our conscious minds, nothing else would matter. We haven't been gifted this beautiful and perfectly balanced plane of reality by some superior and omnipresent deity. But it is because of that force that the potential for the flourishing of life was present at the beginning of it all, why it all could endure in the first place.

You don't need to proclaim everywhere that you are an unrepeatable and blooming flower. Just as you don't need to constantly clarify and assured yourself that you belong to the human race. Whether you like it or not, it is within your nature. And, making the most of that nature and hidden power, is not about standing out from the crowd or being super successful in something in particular. Because, what does 'being successful' mean anyway? As for many other things, it's just an opinion; a consensual and implicit social agreement, usually backed up by the majority of said society, and then taken for granted as an unquestionable truth.

You can have a big house, a successful professional career, or charisma that always brings you to be the centre of attention; but is that what reaching your true potential really means? Just a shaky maybe. As, for some, feeling complete and fulfilled will mean to live the mundane routines of a monotonous life; and being 'on the top of the hill', living a multimillionaire lifestyle will feel empty and hollow. Or completely vice versa. The point is that there are no set cannons separating success from failure that are applicable to everyone.

The only line that separates both exists inside your soul. And absolutely no one else in the world will ever be able to point out whether you are right or wrong about which side of the line your mind-set is falling to. In fact, life is messy and chaotic and most of the time you will be on both sides of the fence simultaneously. It's mostly linked to your own self-awareness, cognitive biases aside, to your ability to understand the path you must follow to fall more often on the 'fulfilled' side of the line.

The game is all about finding meaning and connection, gaining the required awareness to choose what your ultimate and boldest goal is. And, in order to achieve that, you need to understand as many of the mechanisms influencing and interacting with your consciousness as possible: the ones that come easily and intuitively – like our cognitive skills, memory, biological senses, or expectations – and those factors that belong to a very different plane of reality, the Quantum Realm.

Unless you are capable of glimpsing and unleashing the potential that is hidden in that part of your (sub) consciousness – where time, space, and connections happen at a completely different scale – your resources to face those challenges will be handicapped. Furthermore, your possibility of reaching whatever your goal is will be capped. It will be like going into the fight of your life with one hand tied behind your back.

Because the way the world unfolds to us is not purely deterministic and pre-conceived. Although it is true that, for the most part, on the physical side of things, general physical laws and forces like gravity, electromagnetism, etc., stay constant and stable, those time and space limitations are not all that there is. There is a part that unfolds based on probabilities and not certainties, a side of reality that is impacted and shaped by our minds and the Quantum Self. There is a dimension of your consciousness that is connected to a reality where the biological and social rules just don't apply. That place where we all come from, and where we all go to; the one that connects us to everything and everyone throughout life. Because its power, which is our own, is basic, instinctive, and as unavoidable as the forces of gravity, dark matter, or electromagnetism.

But for anything meaningful and worth remembering in life, behind each feeling of accomplishment, experience of peace or satisfaction, united to everything that makes us feel 'alive', adhered to the chunks of our soul that will transcend this world and reality, there will always be a connection to someone that brings that meaning to your existence.

Where would the joy for Copernicus be if he discovered Earth was round, but had lived alone on an isolated island, where no one would ever know about his history-changing discovery? What would be the point of achieving the greatest goal of your life, if there was no one around you to share it with? Can you name any truly meaningful event of your whole life that didn't involve someone else important to you?

If our (sub) consciousness is the centre of this Universe, giving meaning and means for it to exist, in the centre of that centre lie those raw sensations and connections that we establish with the people we care about. That is the real energy source that makes our world and reality spin. That is also why a machine, no matter how well calibrated and designed, will never be able to experience life and its true meaning.

It is something that cannot be explained with words... How do you explain to a computer what love implies and means? How do you program it to feel deception and frustration at the loss of a profound interpersonal connection?

But, just as with time and space, the interpersonal connections we form within our biological and social network, can also be deceiving. Deeply caring for, or even loving someone doesn't automatically mean that all is well. In fact, we take the learned definitions and expectations of each emotion we experience so much for granted, never questioning them for a second. We just assume that love is a good thing because we have been taught so.

But, what about the times when love is understood as toxic behaviour, which brings anxiety and stress to the person experiencing it? You might think "well, that's clearly not love then". However, would you accept someone else telling you what love is and defining which parameters you are allowed to experience love? Absolutely not, because our emotions and the way we perceive the world is our choice. That is the greatest power we all have. Depression is not experiencing constant sadness, but the lack of sensations altogether; the opposite of any feeling is not feeling at all, and that's when your soul starts to vanish.

And, amongst all the emotions holding that inherent power, love is the most meaningful, extreme, subjective and forceful of them all. Its theoretically opposite, hatred, could be the second, but still comes a long way behind – even if we often mix and confuse both. Love is the real engine that motivates and pushes us to aspire for more. It is in the name of love that the greatest accomplishments in history manifest: romantic love, love for any art, love for your country or nation, fraternal love, self-love...

Love is and will always be the most compelling feeling to achieve higher, more permanent and real results, whatever your goal. If the feeling is raw and pure, untainted by the labels we are socially taught, everything you do with love will only generate the kind of energy that allows you to move forward. It is there, when you share that magic energy with someone you truly care about, that you will sense the real connection, leaving a part of your soul anchored in that exact place and moment. In this way, the people you connect with at this quantum level, will always carry a small chunk of your essence, and vice versa, potentially connecting both of you for eternity.

You might surprise the most important person in your world by inviting them to an unforgettable date: the best restaurant in town, great food and wine, amazing views, a smoky desert, and a chilling sensation like you have ever experienced before. However, if it's something you would do repeatedly with anyone, that magic evening would lose its spark. Because it is in the unique shared experiences, with someone you are connected to, that will anchor a small part of each one of you to that magical and unexpected evening, breaking the biological laws of time, space and connection.

The biggest risk comes from mistaking that raw and pure feeling with a similar sensation produced and 'cooked' by your cognitive and biological expectations and limitations. When we desire for more and let our social craving take control of those feelings, the moment of pure magic is contaminated by whichever unrealistic expectations your mind is set to.

Because of this, training that self-awareness on all parts of your consciousness will give you the key to perceive yourself as something bigger than your limitations. Discerning between a true raw moment and connection, and one given by the immediate satisfaction of a social or biological need, will split the difference between who you chose to be in this world, and which version of you is going to transcend after.

Allow yourself to feel freely, beyond the dictatorship of social conventionalisms that command how you should feel or share that connection. Be brave enough to experience your feelings in whichever way makes sense to you and that other person, without rules and limitations. Because this is when you will connect with that part of yourself as old as the Universe itself, your Quantum Self, which flows invisibly through different planes of reality.

Quantum Psychology is not about finding definite answers or ultimate paths towards the Promised Land. There are no takeaways or big lessons that can illuminate or summarise the scope of goodness and rightness in the world. Quantum Psychology is about recognising your ultimate and inherent power, the very same and elementary one that makes us alive. It's about going beyond winning or losing, and towards putting yourself, and those you connect with, in the true centre of this reality.

There is nothing scarier and more beautiful than being vulnerable and exposed, because it is there that you will find meaning and connection with others; it is there that you will strive to grow and become someone bigger than you are now. Anything you do following the instinct of your Quantum Self will always balance you with all the energy around you; from there, you will always win, no matter the final outcome.

So, what's in Quantum Psychology for you? The only thing that always belonged to you, and that no one could give or take from you either. It is your freedom to choose who you want to be in this world; it is your determination to follow a trail where everyone else only sees dust and rocks; it is your conviction about that part of your consciousness connecting you with others; it is the profound instants of meaning that allow us to briefly rule over the incorruptible emperors of time and space.

Because, above all, our existence is a story about time, space, and profound interpersonal connections; concretely about how those three terms, that we take for granted on a daily basis, are deceived by our biological perspective of how we interact with the Universe; even when the truth unfolds right in front of us.

And that, my friend, is why Quantum Psychology implies re-thinking our potential, and our position as conscious beings reining over this version of the Universe.

GLOSSARY

- **Astral projection:** Often understood as the soul leaving the body and travelling beyond the biological limits. From this esoteric perspective, when your soul leaves your body, it is attached to a 'cord', which becomes detached when you die.

- **Big Bang Theory:** The most widely accepted scientific explanation of the origin of the Universe. According to the theory, the early Universe was hot and dense. As time passed, the Universe expanded, cooled, and became less dense.

- **Biocentrism:** They theory that before consciousness, the Universe was just shimmering waves of probability. One of those probabilities created the probability of life, which created consciousness, and

359

consciousness collapsed the Universe's wave state into a physical state.

-       **Cell memory phenomenon:** The phenomenon whereby patients experience personality changes after undergoing organ transplants. The behaviours and emotions acquired by the recipient from the original donor would be explained as combinatorial memories stored in the neurons of the organ donated.

-       **Chakra:** Spiritual energy centres within the human body as described by ancient traditions of Hinduism. Each chakra corresponds to specific organs as well as physical, emotional, psychological, and spiritual states of being that influence all areas of life.

-       **Collective unconscious:** A concept proposed by Carl Jung (1875-1961), it refers to the idea that a segment of the deepest unconscious mind is genetically inherited and is not shaped by personal experience. Jung's theory on the collective unconscious was that it is made up of a collection of knowledge and imagery that every person is born with and is shared by all human beings due to ancestral experience.

-    **Cyclic Universe theory:** A model of cosmic evolution according to which the Universe undergoes endless cycles of expansion and cooling, each beginning with a "big bang" and ending in a "big crunch".

-    **Epigenetics:** The study of the heritable changes in gene expression (active versus inactive genes) that do not involve changes to the underlying DNA sequence – a change in phenotype without a change in genotype – which, in turn, affects how cells read the genes. Epigenetic change is a regular and natural occurrence but can also be influenced by several factors including age, the environment, lifestyle, and disease state.

-    **Feng Shui:** An ancient art and science thought to be the art of placement – understanding how the placement of yourself, and objects within a space, affect your life in various areas of experience. It is a complex body of knowledge that teaches us how to balance and harmonise with the energies in any given space.

-    **Heritability:** The proportion of the total variation between individuals in a given population that is due to genetic variation. It refers to the proportion of variability in a particular trait in a population, explained by differences in the genes.

-       **Hypnosis:** A trance state characterised by extreme suggestibility, relaxation and heightened imagination. It is most often compared to daydreaming, or the feeling of "losing yourself" in a book or movie. You are fully conscious, but you tune out most of the stimuli around you.

-       **Hormones:** Chemical messages or signals that coordinate a range of bodily functions. From the bloodstream, the hormones communicate with the body when they reach their target cell and create a particular change or effect in that cell. The hormone can also create changes in the cells of surrounding tissues.

-       **Immune system:** The body's defense against infectious organisms and other invaders, through a complex and vital network of cells and organs that protect the body from infection. Through a series of steps, called the immune response, the immune system attacks organisms and substances that invade body systems and cause disease. The immune system, although partly innate, also evolves and adapts throughout life.

-   **Interpersonal Entanglement:** Strong and profound personal interconnection between two beings, similarly to the entanglement of subatomic particles in that the subjects can share some properties and feelings that go beyond the biological limitations of macroscopic reality.

-   **Karma:** From a Quantum Psychology perspective, karma can be understood as somewhat of an aggregate of the energetic message we transmit to the world, shaped by our emotions, motivations and happiness. And, just like those, karma is subjective in nature.

-   **Linked Chain Theory:** A conceptual frame describing how different aspects of our existence affect each other, and how either the improvement or the neglect of some factors has consequences on facets of our life that would appear to be unrelated.

-   **Molecular Biology:** The study of biology at a molecular level. Molecular biology chiefly concerns itself with understanding the interactions between the various systems of a cell; including the interrelationship of DNA,

RNA and protein synthesis, and learning how these interactions are regulated.

-   **Multiverse Theory:** The idea that our universe may be one of many (perhaps an infinite number) of alternative universes and that different things may simultaneously happen in each. Therefore, technically everything possible and conceivable might be happening in a parallel universe.

-   **Neurotransmitters:** Chemicals produced by the body that help to coordinate movement and control mood and cognition. They are synthesised by neurons and are stored in vesicles. Neurotransmitters are exchanged in the space between neurons called synapses, and spread out through the nervous system – relaying chemical messages between nerve cells and from neurons to muscles.

-   **Neuro-Linguistic Programming (NLP):** The idea that people operate by internal "maps" of the world that they learn through sensory experiences. NLP tries to detect and modify the unconscious biases or limitations of an individual's map of the world. It operates through the conscious use of language to bring about changes in someone's thoughts and behaviour.

-   **Non-shared environment:** Any aspects of the environment and any experiences that can be different between children within the same family, contributing to differences between family members. Non-shared environment accounts for most environmental influence in psychopathology, personality, and cognitive abilities after adolescence.

-   **Quantum Chemistry:** A branch of chemistry whose primary focus is the application of quantum mechanics in physical models and experiments of chemical systems or molecules.

-   **Quantum computing:** A quantum computer, rather than representing *bits,* uses *qubits*, which can take on the value 0, or 1, or both simultaneously. This parallelism allows a quantum computer to work on a million computations at once, while your desktop computer works on one.

-   **Quantum entanglement:** The ability of subatomic particles to link their properties with one another. When two quantum objects interact in the right way, the information they contain becomes shared. This can result in a kind of connection between those particles, where an action performed on one will automatically affect the nature of the other, even at great distances – perhaps at opposite ends of the Universe.

-   **Quantum tunneling or quantum leap:** The quantum mechanical phenomenon whereby a particle passes through a potential barrier that, according to classical mechanics, it cannot surmount.

-   **Quantum Physics or Quantum Mechanics:** The study of the principles, laws and "behaviours" of the smallest known particles: subatomic particles, which compose and build the entire Universe (from matter, to light, to dark matter, to every single cell in your body).

-   **Quantum Psychology:** The science and theory that studies the nature, implications, and relationships, between the part of our (sub) consciousness (or Quantum Self) governed by the laws of Quantum Mechanics, and how it retro-influences and interacts with our default sensory, cognitive, neuronal, social, and biological mechanisms, including the rest of our (sub) consciousness, which are ruled by the macroscopic or Newtonian physical laws and limited by our biological and social experience of reality.

- **Quantum realm:** All reference to quantum scale phenomena.

- **Quantum Self:** The part of your (sub) consciousness ruled by the laws of Quantum Mechanics and shaped as a result of your interaction and retro-influence between the Quantum Realm and your biological reality mind. It differentiates from Quantum Psychology as the latter also explains the relationships between the former and the Quantum Realm, including in the mix the influence from other links or aspects of your reality contained within the Link Chain Theory.

- **Reiki:** A Japanese technique for stress reduction and relaxation that also promotes healing. It is administered by "laying on hands" and is based on the idea that an unseen "life force energy" flows through us and is what causes us to be alive.

- **Shared environment:** Those aspects of an individual's environment that are necessarily shared with other children in the family, contributing to similarities between family members.

- **Subatomic particle:** Those elements that compose and form an atom, such as neutrons, electrons, protons, and photons, amongst others.

- **Uncertainty principle:** The fundamental notion that we cannot measure the position *and* the momentum of a subatomic particle with absolute precision. The more accurately we know one of these values, the less accurately we know the other.

- **WACO personality pattern:** The personality tendency composed of four personality traits that highly correlate to one another: subjective **W**ell-being, **A**ttributional styles, **C**oping strategies and **O**ptimism.

BE PART OF THE JOURNEY DISCOVERING QUANTUM PSYCHOLOGY!

- **Stay tuned:**

  🌐 TheInvisibleBookOfQuantumPsychology.com

  📘 Facebook.com/SMQuantumPsychology/

  📷 Instagram.com/the.invisible.book.of.qp/

  🐦 Twitter.com/SM68847232

- **Books already for sale:**

👉 The Quantum Pilgrimage:

  An Existential Quest to the Quantum Self

- **Books coming soon:**

👉 The Invisible Book of Quantum Psychology

E-book, paper book and audio book available on Amazon, Barns & Noble and Kobo

Printed in Great Britain
by Amazon